The Maste

(Volume 2)

James Grant

Alpha Editions

This edition published in 2022

ISBN : 9789356908123

Design and Setting By
Alpha Editions
www.alphaedis.com
Email - info@alphaedis.com

Contents

CHAPTER I.

MYSTERY.

So all the guests had quitted Dundargue now but Hawke Holcroft. In two days he was to depart for what he called 'his chambers in town;' thus Allan was compelled to continue his polite dissimulation, and be on suave and apparently easy terms with him as a guest, though the latter felt that there was an undefinable change in his manner towards him.

Indeed, it was only by a great effort of self-control that the Master of Aberfeldie, a man with the highest and keenest sense of honour, and knowing all he did, continued to treat Holcroft with politeness; but he writhed and shivered when he heard him, in the drawing-room or elsewhere, address Olive or Eveline.

All the forenoon after Cameron's departure, when poor little Eveline was most triste and miserable, our other pair of lovers were very happy. They had what they were pleased to call 'a picnic' on the tower-head of Dundargue. Allan's portion thereof was cigars, and Olive's a little basket of purple grapes and luscious strawberries (though the season was autumn) from the hothouses.

So with these two, the hours passed sweetly and swiftly, with the blue sky overhead, while far away in the distance, and steeped in sunny haze, stretched the lovely Carse of Gowrie; and talking of themselves, their past folly, their present joy, and the brilliant future that was to come, they billed and cooed after the fashion of all lovers since flowers grew in Eden.

Allan lolled at length on the stone bartizan of the tower whence molten lead and arrows had more than once been launched on a foe beneath, Olive with her fair head reclined against his shoulder toying with her fruit, while he did so with her silky hair, or kissed her lips and hands, and called her all manner of funny and endearing names that would look rather odd in print; and yet amid their present happiness it was strange that each wondered more than once, if coldness or estrangement would ever come between them again.

Never—oh, never.

'You complained that the gardeners saw me kissing you in the rosery yesterday, Olive,' said Allan. 'Now, little woman, who should I kiss if I don't kiss you? Well, only the crows overhead can see us up here, at all events.'

But now as he toyed with her hands, marvelling as he did so at their whiteness and beauty, and anon played with the bangles that encircled her rounded arms, he bethought of the one worn—yes, actually worn—by Holcroft, and silently he resolved to possess himself of it without delay; so, ere the bell rang for luncheon, he made an excuse, conducted his cousin, with many a pause and long delay which were not idly spent, down the dark and winding staircase from the head of the tower.

In his new-found happiness until now he had forgotten all about the bangle, which—perhaps for some ulterior purpose of his own—Holcroft seemed to have quietly appropriated, and by whom he wished it returned without any fuss or explanation.

To this end he sought that personage after luncheon was over, and was sure he would find him either practising strokes in the billiard-room, in the smoking-room, or stables, watching the horses and catching hints from the grooms.

He found him in the first-named place, cue in hand.

'Ready for a game?' said he.

'No, thanks.'

'Sorry; Cameron, and everyone is gone. I'm reduced to playing the right hand against the left.'

'And while playing I perceive that you have a gold bangle of Miss Raymond's on your left wrist?'

'Yes,' replied Holcroft, leisurely—Allan thought impertinently.

'Did she give it to you?'

'Why do you ask?'

'*Did* she give it to you?' repeated Allan, with a dangerous gleam in his dark eyes.

'No.'

'How comes it to be there, then?'

'Don't take to high falutin. I slipped it on in mere fun, and it will not come off again.

'Indeed! allow me.'

And Allan, in a moment, by twisting the ductile Indian gold, wrenched it off, and Holcroft's eyes had a malevolent flash in them as he stooped to strike a ball.

'Thanks,' said Allan, pocketing the bangle. 'Now we shall have a cigar.'

For a moment he felt a little ashamed of his sudden irritation, and proffered his cigar-case to Holcroft, who smiled his thanks and accepted a Havana.

The Master was younger and handsomer than he; the heir to an ancient title and estate; he had the envied prestige of having borne himself bravely when under fire with the Black Watch, and had a goodly crop of medals—not so many as my Lord Wolseley, of course—but still, when in uniform, a goodly display.

He had all the advantages over Hawke Holcroft that one man could have over another; and in his heart of hearts the other hated—yea, with a bitter and deadly hate—Allan Graham—a hate beyond his love, real or supposed, for Olive Raymond, natheless all Olive's beauty and her money—his chief lure and incentive.

While conversing and joking together in the smoking-room, or on the terrace, amid the pleasures of the table, knocking the balls about at billiards or so forth, how little could the unconscious Allan have dreamed that his father's guest—the son of his old friend—had been pondering over the art of 'Killing no murder;' of accidents brought about in the hunting-field, at cover shooting, or hill-climbing; even of dynamite cigars! Had he not heard of such things at Monaco, Homburg, and elsewhere.

He knew that there was quite a manufactory of such cigars at Temeswar, in Austria; but wherever were such pleasant gifts 'to be obtained in an out-of-the-way hole like the Carse of Gowrie?'

His teeth under his moustache glittered or glistened whitely when such ideas occurred to him; though he chatted away with perhaps forced *insouciance* and gaiety, under all his assumed ease of manner there smouldered a lava-like glow—mingled hate of Allan and coveting of Olive, but with an emotion of a much coarser nature, combined with greed.

Seeing Clairette, Olive's maid, passing, Allan made up the bangle in a little packet as he still wished no more explanations on the subject, and desired her to give it to her mistress.

'You and Miss Raymond seem exceedingly good friends now,' said Holcroft.

'We were never otherwise,' replied Allan, curtly, and displeased by the remark.

'What a prize in matrimony such a girl must be, with so much beauty and—wealth.'

'It is sometimes a misfortune for a girl to be rich, or to be thought so,' said Allan.

'Why?'

'Because she may become the prey of some needy fortune-hunter or enterprising scamp.'

Holcroft winced at the reply, though it was made casually and without the least design by Allan.

'But in marrying, Miss Raymond might perhaps be poor enough.'

'What paradox is this?' asked Holcroft, thoroughly interested, while Allan felt some disdain at discussing such matters with such a man.

'Yes, poor as a church mouse, unless—'

'Unless what?'

'She marries *me*,' replied Allan, who, with perhaps pardonable pique, only thought of provoking a man who had tried to rival him, and whom he deemed a needy and adventurous gambler.

This seemed only to corroborate what Holcroft had heard before, and gave him some occasion for thought.

'I have heard rumours of a family compact—a most fortunate one for you,' said he, smiling; 'but suppose you—excuse me for saying so—were to predecease her?'

'Then my pretty cousin would be a free woman; but I don't mean to die yet awhile. Let us take a turn before dinner,' he added, to change the conversation he had no desire to continue.

'Where?'

'Anywhere you like; but, as the evening has become chill, suppose we smoke our cigars in the picture-gallery?'

'All right, I am your man.'

Had Allan looked at Hawke Holcroft just then he might have perceived a lurid gleam in his stealthy eyes, and how his hands were clenched till the nails of his fingers bruised the palms thereof.

Olive received her bangle, and though startled by the abruptness with which it was returned, without message or explanation from Allan, as Clairette told her, she thought less of the circumstance then than she did a day or two after.

Dinner was announced; Holcroft appeared in accurate evening dress as usual, and, after waiting a few minutes for Allan who did not appear, the meal was proceeded with in the slow fashion peculiar to Dundargue, though only five were seated at table.

Ere dessert came, Lady Aberfeldie dispatched a servant to Allan's room in search of him. He was not there, though his evening dress was laid out as usual.

'Where can he be? Where can he have gone?' were the queries on all hands, which, as night began to draw on without his appearing, took the form of alarm, 'and what can have happened?'

'Did Allan drop hints of going anywhere?' asked Lord Aberfeldie.

All answered 'No.'

'It is most mysterious.'

Still more mysterious did it appear when the night, passed without his being seen, and when his place was still vacant at the breakfast-table next day. Lord Aberfeldie was in dire perplexity; the ladies were pale and already betook themselves to tears.

'If Allan has left the house as suddenly as he did before, he has taken neither clothes nor portmanteau with him, as Tappleton assures me; so what can it mean?' exclaimed Lord Aberfeldie.

A gun was missing from the gun-room. Could Allan have gone to shoot with Logan at Loganlee? But Olive deemed it impossible that he would do so without consulting her, and on looking at Holcroft she thought he looked rather hot and disturbed.

'The bangle, the bangle!' thought the girl, with sudden terror. 'Can he have gone in a fit of jealousy. Mercy! if it should be so.'

Inquiries proved that Allan had not passed out by the entrance gates, as the lodge-keeper affirmed, and no trace of footsteps could be found at any of the private gates to the grounds; and it was soon discovered that he had not taken a ticket for any place at the railway station.

What terrible mystery was here?

The family began to look with growing alarm and dismay blankly into each other's pale faces.

Keepers and gillies, strong, active, and keen-sighted fellows, Hector, Alister Bain, Angus and Dugal Glas—even old Ronald Gair, the piper—searched, but in vain, the grounds, plantations, even the adjacent hills and glens; but not a trace was found of the missing Allan.

He seemed suddenly to have dropped out of existence.

As this, his last day at Dundargue, drew on, none made himself more active in searching and riding about the roads than Holcroft, and so preoccupied were all that no one—even Olive—noticed that his face was pale and cadaverous—and wore a very disturbed expression, and that his pale eyes seemed to glare defiantly if anyone looked at him, while he sedulously kept his *right hand gloved.*

How are we to relate all that really had happened.

CHAPTER II.

A MODERN USE FOR A MEDIÆVAL INSTITUTION.

'The world is not a bad world, after all,' said Allan, as he and Holcroft, after a casual glance at the long lines of portraits panelled in the wainscotting of the gallery, together with many a Cuyp, Zucchero, Canaletti, and so forth, now looked out from one of the lofty windows upon the fair domain of his family, that spread for miles around Dundargue.

'It is easy enough for you to talk thus of the world,' thought Holcroft, 'but if, like me, you had only debts and difficulties for your patrimony you might take a different view.'

'I was born here in Dundargue, and all the happy memories of my childhood centre round it,' said Allan. 'Every man, woman, and child in the place are known to me; every rock and hill, glen and woodland, familiar, with all their stories and traditions; and wherever I might be with the Black Watch, in England on the staff, far away in central India, or in the gorges of Afghanistan, my memory always fled home to dear old Dundargue and all its surroundings.'

'How pathetic!' sneered Holcroft, silently, and puzzled to understand the mood of Allan, who, in the consciousness of his own happiness with Olive, felt at that moment rather inclined to take a soft and generous view of the world at large.

'It certainly is a fine old ancestral house—one to be proud of,' said Holcroft, aloud, 'with a special history, and all that sort of thing. I have heard a devil of a deal about its oubliette—where is it?'

'Let me show you—come this way,' said Allan, lighting a fresh cigar.

Smoking together, Allan, and Holcroft following, wandered up and down circular stone stairs in narrow turrets, where the steps had been worn and hollowed by the feet of long departed generations; through dusky corridors where, in some places, moth-eaten arras hung upon its rusty tenter-hooks, and where, as Holcroft said, there was 'a loud smell of mice;' through secret doors and past 'the priest's hole,' in which James of Jerusalem abode, till they reached a narrow stone passage near the summit of the great tower, closed by a massive little door.

Allan threw this open, and the black, round mouth of the oubliette, about four feet in diameter, yawned before them.

The great, horizontal stone slab or flagstone, which in ancient times had closed the mouth of this horrible accessory to feudal tyranny, had long since given place to a massive trap-door of oak, which was held up by a wooden prop, under which the cold, dark vault showed its mysterious profundity.

'By Jove! it is a strange affair; more like a draw-well than anything else.'

'But supposed to be twelve feet diameter at the bottom—a fine old relic of the days when "warriors bold wore spurs of gold," and the rack and the red-hot ploughshare were aids to the orthodox opinions of society in religion and politics.'

And Allan laughed as he spoke.

'How foetid its atmosphere is! That door has not been open for an age, and may be closed for as long again. No one ever comes here.'

Peering downward, as if into a well, they saw the outlines of their heads reflected in a little pool of water at the bottom, but how far down it was impossible to say.

'Once upon a time,' said Allan, 'when parts of the Carse of Gowrie were under water, in wet seasons especially, it flowed in here, how no one knew, unless through fissures in the rock, and drowned like a rat any luckless wight who was thrown in to be—to be——'

'What?'

'Forgotten. So the phrase went then; hence its name.'

'And do you mean to say that no one who was dropped into that confounded hole ever came up again?'

'Yes.'

'Were their cries not heard?'

'No; the walls around are so thick, and the bottom is in the living rock on which Dundargue stands.'

'By Jove!' exclaimed Holcroft again, as if perplexed, so much so that he had let his cigar grow cold. 'And their bones?' he asked, after a pause.

'Were found in quantities by certain explorers, who went down with torches, some years ago. I have not looked into this place for years—not since I left for the regiment in India,' said Allan, stooping, somewhat dangerously—and, to Holcroft's sudden idea, somewhat temptingly—over the dangerous profundity, into which he was striving to peer.

With all the rapidity of light, many terrible thoughts now crowded into the mind of Holcroft. He hated Allan Graham with deadly rivalry and hate combined. Never again, in the desperation of his affairs, might he have the chance of an introduction to such a prize as Olive Raymond, or be on such a footing, as he had recently found himself with her.

He loathed Allan for all Allan possessed, and, as we are told, 'a coward who knows himself to be at once despised but unchastised, for a woman's sake, can hate.'

If he lost his chances with Olive, beggary stared him in the face; drops of perspiration started to his forehead, and chance now confirmed his diabolical resolution. The gloomy fiend was uppermost, his revenge, and perhaps future triumph, stood embodied before him. He did not pause, and all these dire thoughts occurred to him in less than the space of one vibration of a pendulum.

Had the Master of Aberfeldie turned sharply round he might have read in Holcroft's white face an expression that was not pleasant to look upon just then—the face of one that would work him mischief if he could; but the unwitting Allan was doing what he had not done since boyhood, he was peering with vague curiosity into the profundity below.

A fury, a clamorous anxiety, seemed to blaze up in the heart and brain of Holcroft, who was a practised 'bruiser,' and he suddenly gave Allan an awful blow under the left ear—a blow hit right out from the shoulder—that shot him headlong into the vault.

He vanished from the light; there was a heavy thud far down below, and then all became still—unnaturally so; but Holcroft could hear the beating of his own pulses, while the blood seemed to be surging about his throbbing temples.

Was he acting in a dream from which he would waken to find himself in bed? or was all this happening, not to him, but to some one else? No, there was the bruised right hand, from which the violence of his blow had torn the skin.

He had read of dark crimes, of *murders*, but little did he think he would ever become the participator in such a deed; but opportunity is always the devil's game.

For a minute—an eternity it seemed, by the chaos of his mind, the sudden inversion of all thought—he did not breathe, he scarcely seemed to live.

There was a whisper of 'murder' on his lips, and it seemed to have an echo, that terrible whisper, but whether from the walls, the trees that waved below them, the blue sky, or the crows that were winging their way through it, he knew not. He seemed to whisper the awful word to himself, with quivering lips, again and again, as if he required an assurance of its truth, and then sought to rouse himself from his lethargic stupor, quit the scene of his sudden crime, and seek safety in flight—flight!

But, then, to quit Dundargue thus would fix suspicion on himself. Had not Clairette, the French maid, seen him but lately with Allan? And flight would mar the very object for which he had committed the crime.

Should he—could he—at all risks to himself and his fortune, ere it was too late, strive to undo what he had done; to give an alarm, and make some excuse or explanation ere life had departed from the shattered frame of his victim, or leave the latter to his obscure fate—a grave under his father's roof!

Cowardice and meanness, hatred, jealousy, and avarice all suggested the latter.

He knew not the depth of this strange prison, or how far down beneath the foundations of lofty Dundargue and into the rock on which it stands, the sill or floor of the noisome vault might be.

He listened; not a sound came upward, nor was there any, save the wild beating of his own heart and the buzzing and singing of blood in his ears.

He softly closed the wooden trap-door, let the enormous iron hasp thereof drop over the rusty staple; he closed the massive external entrance, and stealthily crept or glided away.

There seemed a silence all around him now; such a silence as must have appalled the soul of the first murderer when he 'rose up against Abel, his brother, and slew him.'

So the tragedy—the dark crime—was acted as suddenly as it was weird—suggested by a whisper of the devil! There was nothing very tragic in the accessories of the scene; but, as an author says, 'Are not real tragedies, the social tragedies that go on about us in our every-day life, enacted like comedies, until the last moment, when the curtain falls, and all is dark?'

Pale as death in visage (he felt himself to be so), stealthy in step and eye, he stole away to his own apartment in a modern part of the mansion. How he reached it he never knew, but mechanically of course, and he blessed his stars that he reached it unseen.

He took a long pull at the brandy flask—tore off his collar and necktie, and cast himself half fainting on his bed, where he lay panting and gasping heavily.

Every sound that came to his ear, every step that approached, seemed to Hawke Holcroft the herald of discovery, and he longed with the most intense nervous intensity to leave this loathed Dundargue behind him!

Was the Master dying there or dead outright? Where he lay no sound could ever reach the external air. But had not his victim assured him that no cry could ever come from there—the place was so deep—so remote?

Would the next evening, when he was to depart, never come? Then he had the meals, the family, and their surmises to face!

He had a haggard and hunted look that evening and all next day, which Lord Aberfeldie, in the kindness of his heart, amid all his own new anxiety, attributed to the pressure of his monetary affairs.

CHAPTER III.

HOLCROFT DEPARTS.

It was a considerable relief to Holcroft's mind to perceive that this second abrupt disappearance of Allan excited more surprise than alarm in his family circle; and in her own thoughts Lady Aberfeldie secretly connected it with some lovers' quarrel between him and Olive; it was so like their past relations that some such folly should intervene.

The bell for dinner sounded much earlier than usual, as Mr. Holcroft was to depart for the south that evening, and to see him in the drawing-room dressed *de rigueur* in black, with spotless shirt-front and diamond studs, with tie and collar perfect, his hair brushed with precision and the ends of his tawny moustache waxed out to sharp points, who could have imagined him an actor in that scene in the distant arched passage, or connected him with what was lying at the bottom of that deep, dark oubliette!

Holcroft always thought that great games involved serious hazards; but now this was a hazard beyond all his previous calculations.

The greatest chance of fortune he had ever seen in his varied life seemed to be slipping—or to have speedily slipped—away from him, when Olive Raymond and her cousin suddenly appeared on such amicable terms; savage emotions of mingled disappointment and revenge filled his heart, and certainly he had given full swing to them!

Now, what he had done was over; the rubicon had been passed. He was—what he dared not name himself: the thought of all that Allan Graham must endure ere he died (if he was not already dead) was—at times, but at times only—maddening even to his destroyer; and he felt that he could not too soon place miles upon miles between himself and Dundargue; and that, happen what might, he would never set foot in Dundargue again.

Seated at that luxurious table with the hospitable father, the patrician-like mother, the tender sister and brilliant *fiancée* of him he had slain, with stately-liveried valets in attendance, while longing for the conveyance or carriage that was to take him to the station, he *did* feel more than once as if he would go mad if it lasted much longer—this acting—this tension of the heart—but, as we say, for a time only. He was too near the scene of his awful crime not to feel his soul shrink with selfish horror and dismay, which made him nervously twist up, roll, and unroll his *serviette*, as it is called in Scotland.

Was it only a few hours since he had heard that terrible *thud* amid the darkness and the clash of the oak trap-door? And there were *his* family all seated with him—Holcroft—at the same table, all unconscious of what was lying within a few yards of them, and yet not considering him the blackest criminal in the world, but a departing guest to be treated with kindness and courtesy.

Thank heaven he would be far away from them ere Allan would be found to be hopelessly gone, and he would see nothing of their growing misery.

To drown thought, care, and memory, Holcroft, after the ladies retired to the drawing-room, imbibed systematically more than usual. Ere this, Olive had thought his manner excited—strange only. Unused to see men under the influence of wine, she thought no more of it. But, as Holcroft took to 'lacing' his clicquot with brandy when occasion served, that may account for some of the peculiar remarks to Olive yet to be recorded.

From an early period Eveline had conceived a shuddering kind of aversion of Holcroft—an emotion not rare in certain nervous organisations like hers; nor could she have explained why more particularly *now* his presence, though at table as usual, had filled her with an undefined distrust and dread; yet so it was.

But in the drawing-room her own thoughts came more than ever back to her, and these were all of Evan Cameron.

'He is gone!' she was always whispering to herself; 'too probably for ever and for ever. We shall never meet again. How dull my world will seem without Evan, and how old and queer I begin to feel already!'

But poor Eveline knew not what a small place the world is—now-a-days especially.

'You seem rather out of sorts,' said Lord Aberfeldie, who had been eyeing 'his old friend's son,' while pushing the decanters towards him; 'I hope there is nothing wrong with you, especially as this is your last evening here.'

'No, nothing very wrong,' stammered Holcroft, scarcely knowing what to say, but driven to shelter himself under what was his normal condition; 'it is only—only——'

'What?'

'I have had more than one annoying letter,' he said, with a kind of gasp, and paused.

'About money—of course?' said Lord Aberfeldie.

'One was a threat from a tailor,' replied Holcroft, making a terrible effort to appear facetious, 'who says if I don't pay him he will take means to make me do so.'

'And you?'

'Wrote back that I was delighted to hear he had the means, as this was more than I had.'

'Well, my dear fellow, your father was one of my oldest friends; for his sake can I square it for you?'

'Oh, Lord Aberfeldie, don't think of that!'

'What's the total?" asked the other, opening a davenport.

'Close on £500,' said Holcroft, with an effort, which certainly was an emotion, but not gratitude.

'There, Holcroft—pay me when you can, or choose,' said Lord Aberfeldie, throwing down his pen, closing the davenport, and handing a cheque for the sum named to his guest, to stop whose thanks he plunged at once into the inevitable story of the charge of the Black Watch along the Kourgané Hill; how he fell wounded; and how, but for Holcroft's father, 'a squad of infernal Russians,' *et cetera*, and so forth.

'Another glass of Moët, and then we shall join the ladies.'

'Life is a hard game with some of us now,' said Holcroft, as he pocketed his cheque. 'As some one has written, "Men cannot go freebooting or looting now, except in business; and it is quite a question whether a modern *promoter* is not quite as respectable a member of society as a riever used to be, in the old days when right was might."

'And Dundargue was built,' added Lord Aberfeldie, laughing.

'I did not say so.'

'Ah, but you thought it.'

And now they rose from the table.

Holcroft was not the better, but rather the worse for his potations. He had eaten little and drunk much. Thus he looked very pale—almost ghastly; and a strange fixed grimness replaced occasionally the usual restlessness of his shifty pale eyes and freckled face.

Curiously enough he had hovering in his mind a kind of vengeance just then at Olive. But for her sudden, and, as he thought, capricious preference for her cousin, and throwing *him* so completely over, the deed he had committed would never have been done.

Eveline had withdrawn to her room, whither her mother had followed her, bent on worry and expostulation no doubt; Lord Aberfeldie was required by his steward, and Holcroft found Olive seated alone in a bay window of the drawing-room, watching the last rays of the sun fading out behind the Sidlaw Hills.

'Another hour—even less, Miss Raymond—and my place here will be vacant,' said he, in a low and unnatural voice, while attempting to hang over her chair in his old fashion.

'I got back my bangle, thanks,' said she, a little irrelevantly, but feeling a necessity for saying something.

'Have you forgotten all that passed between us before and after you allowed me to retain it.'

'I never allowed you to retain it, nor aught of mine, save perhaps a bud from a bouquet. I have not forgotten that you, apparently, sought to do me a great honour, Mr. Holcroft; but I scarcely thought, even then, that you were serious.'

'Serious! Did you not know that I loved you better than my own life.'

'I cannot listen to this kind of thing,' said she, rising with positive hauteur and annoyance in her face and manner; 'you forget yourself.'

'When with you I always do—forgive me!'

'I cannot forgive you for talking to me thus.'

'You used not to dislike me, I know; and now there is no sacrifice I would not make to win your love——'

'Permit me to pass!' exclaimed Olive, but he barred her way, and now a glow of half-tipsy rage seemed to possess him.

'Listen, Olive Raymond,' said he, in a low, concentrated and almost fierce tone; 'I have dared and risked much for you—more than you can conceive. There has seldom been aught that I have sworn to possess that has not in time been mine—mine, do you hear! To those who wait, their time and turn always come. I have sworn to possess you, and woe to the man who comes between us.'

She regarded him with a haughty and scared yet scornful eye. She saw now that this melo-drama was the result of wine.

'Do you think you could compel me to love you?' she asked, with a provoking smile.

'No.'

'What then?'

'To marry me.'

'Under what pressure, sir?'

'That is my secret—-in time you may find it out,' he added, bowing to her with ominous, not mock, politeness, as she passed him with a haughty stare, and left the room. 'She forgets that I have yet her photo, with her own name written on the back in her own hand; and if ever man put the screw on a woman by such a little thing as that, I shall put it on you, Olive Raymond, if you continue to play my Lady Disdain to me!'

And for a moment he cast after her retiring figure a glance of sardonic hate a devil might have emulated.

'Good-bye,' he muttered, mockingly, 'is an unpleasant thing to say; with us let it be *au revoir* rather; perhaps she may yet wave a damp pocket-handkerchief from the outward wall as I ride away; who knows.'

'Sorry to say time is up, my dear fellow,' said Lord Aberfeldie, entering the room with his hat and driving gloves; 'make your adieux to the ladies. There is little doubt that Allan has gone to Loganlee—the covers are first-rate there. I'll just drive over and see, dropping you and your traps at the railway station *en passant*.'

A few minutes more and the pair were tooling down the avenue in a smart mail phaeton, drawn by a pair of fine, high-stepping dark greys. So Lord Aberfeldie drove 'the son of his oldest friend' to the station, and, as the distance increased between himself and Dundargue, Holcroft's spirits revived, as if nothing had happened there at all; he actually said,

'And you think to find Allan at Loganlee?'

'I haven't a doubt of it—some tift with Olive, no doubt.'

'*Au revoir*, Lord Aberfeldie! and a thousand thanks for all your kindness to me—never shall forget it, by Jove! but I shall have the pleasure of seeing you all again in town, of course.'

To this expression of pleasure Lord Aberfeldie made no response, but shook Holcroft's hand, whipped up his greys, and was off, thinking,

'I am glad *he* has gone; he looks sadly strange and queer, poor fellow.'

Holcroft was intensely relieved when the peer had left, and, making straight for the railway buffet, imbibed glass after glass of pretty potent Glenlivat, conversing affably the while with the young damsel thereat.

'Of what are you thinking, sir, that you stare at me so?' she asked, with a giggle.

'Only that your mother must have been a sweetly pretty girl!'

The train was late; thus he had to spend some time in staring aimlessly at the flaming advertisements on the station wall—an Anglo-American fashion now spread to Scotland—advertisements of some one's cocoa, some one's corsets, some one's whisky, and so forth; and, after glancing with a contemptuous malediction at the thick bible left by the Scottish something society in the little waiting-room, he smoked a cigar, had himself weighed, had a brandy and soda, had some more chaff with the pretty girl at the buffet, till the night train came snorting and clanking in, when he took his seat, spread his rugs, and was off, as he thought, to security at last!

Though he was not without reasonable and selfish dread for the future, as the night train sped on its swift way, and left the Carse of Gowrie far behind, he felt no genuine compunction for the atrocity he had committed.

He did not possess a single spark of honour, gratitude, compunction, or compassion. By unfair play he had rooked many; he had hocussed horses; and once ruined a poor lad in the Lancers, on whom he contrived to cast the suspicion of his own act. The Lancer was dismissed the service by sentence of a court-martial, and shot himself next day; and Hawke Holcroft took his luxurious luncheon quietly in the same inn where the inquest was held, at the same time. He had extorted money in many ways—he had never precisely robbed; but never before had he been in the dark abyss of assassination and death till now!

The annals of our courts of justice contain many a terrible tale of guilt; but, says a novelist with truth, these would appear like nothing with the history of undiscovered and unpunished crime. 'The assassin who accomplishes his terrible purpose so craftily as to escape detection is a cool and calculating fiend, by the side of whose supreme villainy, the half-premeditated crime of the ordinary shedder of blood, is dwarfed into insignificance.'

So on and on sped the swift night train, and there seemed every probability that the deed of Holcroft would be one of the crimes referred to, that are neither discovered nor punished.

He gave a last look into his pocket-book to assure himself that the cheque and the photo of Olive were safe, and then tried to compose himself to sleep.

Let us hope that the attempt was vain!

He could not help pondering over the remark of Allan about how foetid the air of the oubliette was—that the door had not been opened for an age, and no one ever thought of going near it.

CHAPTER IV.

SUSPENSE.

Lord Aberfeldie drove home in some alarm and dismay. Allan was not at Loganlee, nor had he been near it! When Ruby, the amber-haired little beauty, heard of his visit and its object, she was not slow to connect Allan's second disappearance with some lover's quarrel between him and Olive, and to gather certain jealous and pleasant hopes therefrom, for Allan was decidedly 'a weakness' of Ruby's.

Uncertainty and suspense were increasing now in all their minute horror at Dundargue; while surmises proved endless, futile, and unavailing.

He was gone—but where, or how, and why?

'Something has happened—something fatal—to my son!' wailed Lady Aberfeldie. 'Give me back those fatal diamonds, Eveline. They are never worn, that sorrow does not come to Dundargue!'

'Take courage, my lady,' said old Tappleton, the butler; 'ill news aye travels fast enough, and if ought was wrang wi' the Master, we should hae heard o't ere now.'

Evan Cameron, now with his regiment, and the legal agents of the family at Edinburgh, were alike perplexed on the receipt of letters from Lord Aberfeldie inquiring anxiously if they knew anything of the movements of Allan, and both telegraphed back that they could give no information on the subject.

With these telegrams the last hope passed away, and when the third day of his disappearance began to close a kind of horror seemed to settle over the household, and again a general, and, of course, unavailing, search was made through the entire neighbourhood.

On the face of the servants, male and female, there was never a smile now, as they all loved Allan well; it was no assumed expression they wore; but they went about their daily work with a hushed and subdued air as if there was death in the house, and they fully felt the weight of the mystery.

And ever at table stood the vacant chair, while covers were laid as usual for the absent one.

An accident must have happened; but of what nature? Lord Aberfeldie was beginning to think grimly, vaguely, and painfully of the future. If aught fatal had happened to Allan—his only son—an idea from which his soul shrunk—his cherished title and the grand old house of Dundargue would pass to a remote cousin, one who, by long residence in England, by intermarriage there, by training, breeding, and habit of thought, cared no more for Scotland and her interests, or for the traditions of the Grahams of Aberfeldie, than for those of Timbuctoo.

Such ideas and fears had occurred to him once before, he could remember, when Allan's name appeared among the list of severely wounded in that episode of the Afghan affair, which won him the Victoria Cross.

To Lady Aberfeldie, such ideas, if they occurred at all, were minor indeed to the memories of Allan as the babe she had nursed in her bosom, and the curly-haired boy who had prattled at her knee; and on whom, in manhood and his prime, she had gazed with such maternal pride and admiration when she saw him with the tartan and plumed bonnet, in all the bravery of the Black Watch.

As for poor Olive and Eveline they could only weep together from time to time in all the girlish abandonment of woe.

So hour by hour the silent time stole on at Dundargue.

Till now Olive had never known how deeply and truly she loved Allan, of the hold his image had upon her heart; and how she had repented the pain her petulance must have cost him.

Her eyes in the morning light looked weary, and yet there was an unnatural sparkle in that weariness; her rich brown hair, to the dismay of Mademoiselle Clairette, was left almost undressed, and was pushed back from her throbbing temples; her lips, though scarlet still, looked hard, dry, and cracked, while the whole expression of her face seemed changed.

What was to be the clue, if ever there would be one, to this dreadful mystery!

Meanwhile it might be inquired by the reader whether Mr. Hawke Holcroft was troubled by his conscience. He certainly never betrayed any outward signs thereof—though conscience has been described as making cowards of us all—but he was not without certain reasonable and wholesome fears of discovery and connection of the crime with himself.

He was far away from Dundargue and all its influences. In fact, it seemed a kind of dream to him the circumstance of ever having been there at all; and as weeks passed on nothing could exceed his perplexity and astonishment, though located in an obscure corner of London to avoid his creditors and, *pro tem.*, everyone else, to hear nothing of the affair at Dundargue or of the Master being missing.

Sedulously he searched the daily prints, sedulously he watched the sensational portions of the evening third and fourth editions, but the matter was never referred to. No advertisements appeared offering rewards; no detectives, or the usual machinery seemed to have been put in motion. What could it all mean—this silence and mystery?

Everything however trivial finds its way into print now, and the son of a peer—and an officer in Her Majesty's service, too—does not vanish every day!

At last he got a shock, when a poster proclaimed in large capitals '*The mysterious outrage at Dun*—' but his sight failed him for a moment, and when again he looked he perceived that it was not Dundargue, but 'Dunecht,' that was mentioned with reference to the affair of a past time.

But in all this we are somewhat anticipating.

CHAPTER V.

THE OUBLIETTE.

In these unromantic, plodding, prosaic days of railways, telegraphs, and telephones who would imagine that the fine old family mansion of Dundargue would be the scene of a crime—of a tragedy—suited only to the days of the Sir Malise Graham of the fourteenth century?

Yet so it was.

Allan was not killed—he was perhaps one of those fellows who are not easily killed—but he was severely injured by the fall and concussion, and it was long before he began to struggle back into a consciousness of existence, as he had fallen partly on his head and left shoulder.

The former had suffered from that circumstance, and from the dreadful blow dealt him by Hawke Holcroft; and he was not slow in discovering that his left arm was useless—broken above the elbow.

'Thank heaven, it is not my sword arm!' he whispered, huskily, as he strove to stagger up; but only to sink helplessly down again on the cold stone floor of his prison.

He was too weak—too confused to feel either just rage or indignation yet. There was a horrible dream-like sense of utter unreality in the whole situation in which he so suddenly found himself, and some time elapsed before the whole episode with Holcroft—his unfortunate offer to show him this fatal place, the situation and character of which had suddenly suggested the crime—their idling in the picture-gallery, smoking and wandering through corridors, up and down ancient stairs, with eventually a sudden recollection of the whole adventure—surged into his brain, and a gasp of rage escaped him.

'Accursed coward and villain!' muttered Allan, looking upward; but all was darkness there and around him.

The hours stole on. He staggered up, and at last began to explore the place in which he found himself—a somewhat needless act, as he knew it but too well, having many a time, when a boy, with fear, awe, and curiosity, lowered down a candle at the end of a string, and seen it swaying to and fro far down below till the damp vapour extinguished the flame.

Yet he felt with his right hand the circular wall of massive masonry which enclosed him, carefully again and again, in the desperate hope of finding some outlet, though he knew well by the history and traditions of the place that no such thing could ever have existed; but he could not remain still or withstand the nervous desire for exertion—to be up and doing something; till again he sank on the floor in utter weariness of heart, albeit that heart was aflame with rage.

He uttered shouts for help from time to time, till his voice became hoarse and began to fail him, and his spirit too, as he knew the enormous thickness of the old walls around him; and tears of rage almost escaped him as he pondered over the cold and calculating villainy, of which he was now so mysteriously the helpless victim.

He had no doubt that the hours of the night were now stealing on, and that long ere this his absence must have been discovered, and speculation would be rife. He had his watch, but he was in utter and blackest darkness, and his box of cigar lights having dropped from his pocket he had no means of consulting the dial.

He could but lie there in great pain and passive misery—a misery that seemed so unnatural that it was like a nightmare, an unreality, that must pass away as suddenly as it had come upon him.

How terrible and indescribable, however, grew his aching thoughts as the weary time went on!

He might die of cold, of hunger, of agony—die within a few yards of his own hearthstone—die thus under his father's roof, and close by where at that very moment the whole family were a prey to bewilderment and distress by his sudden disappearance!

Oh, it was all too maddening to think of. So there he could but lie, buried, immured, entombed in darkness; chill as death, not a breath of pure air in his nostrils; not the faintest glimmer of light, and no human sound in his ears. As the hours crept on he could scarcely distinguish waking from sleeping, a dream from reality; and at times all seemed to become chaos, and he could think of nothing unless it were a buzzing in his head and the acute agony of his broken arm.

Anon he would utter a feeble shout for 'help,' but his own voice seemed to return to him; beyond the walls that enclosed him it would not go. He knew that there are situations in life incident to misery and painful excitement, when the human machinery by the rapidity of mental action is worn out sooner than its alloted time, and he began to consider how long it was possible to exist without food or water.

Wearily, agonisingly the hours dragged on.

By this time he was certain that night had passed and day had come again; and what must the thoughts of his people be? Inquiries and searches would be made he knew, but who would ever dream of searching for him where he was *then.*

He had not yet begun to suffer from hunger, but he had a considerable thirst, and hunger would come too.

He thought of all he had read of the endurance of men on rafts and in open boats at sea; of entombed miners buried deep in the bowels of the earth, and his hair seemed to bristle up at the recollections. Hunger, thirst, and an unknown death—or death at such craven hands.

'Oh, God,' he moaned, 'will aid never—never come?'

In that gruesome place and time there occurred to him—ghastly memory!—thoughts of the unknown and forgotten dead whose matted bones had been found in it by antiquarian explorers, as he had mentioned to Holcroft—the remains of unfortunate creatures flung in there by his forefathers.

Could it be that this unlooked-for fate of his was to be a species of expiation for them? And was he to die now by this death, when life had become to him so much dearer than ever?

If his disappearance remained utterly unaccounted for, and his death became—as of course it would be—a thing of the past, and forgotten even by those to whom he was dear, might not Hawke Holcroft regain such influence as he had ever possessed over Olive and make her his own? She would be free then; there would be no obstacle, and no other rendering of the will necessary, now that *he* was removed.

Never again to see her face or the faces of those he loved and who loved him so; to die a rat's death, within arm's length of them almost! Could his ancestor have foreseen, when he formed this infernal trap, that one of his own race was to perish therein, and thus!

After a time, amid all this tangle of terrible thoughts, he began to forget where he was; his senses partly left him; he believed himself to be with the regiment—the Black Watch, with their dark tartans and historic crimson plumes; he heard the crash of the drums, the braying of the pipes, and saw many familiar faces around him, those of Cameron and Carslogie among others. Now the regiment was going into action; he saw the line forming, the eyes of the men lighting grimly up as they loaded, and the sunshine flashed upon the ridges of levelled steel. The dream seemed a palpable one, and, with a shout louder than he thought he could utter, he called upon them to follow him in the charge!

His own cry awoke or roused him; the glorious vision of the charging line melted into opaque darkness, and now Allan found himself weaker than ever. He thought all was nearly over with him now. He turned his thoughts to prayer, ere it might be too late, and from pondering on release and vengeance and the things of this life, he began to think, as his powers ebbed, of the life to come.

He felt that he must resign himself to the inevitable, and to die—to die there after all, and at last he became totally insensible.

CHAPTER VI.

CEAD MILLE MALOCH!

The shout uttered by Allan in his delirium had not been uttered in vain.

It chanced that Mr. Tappleton, the silver-haired old butler, who had been custodier of the wine binns and the massive old plate in its iron-bound chest, since the present Lord Aberfeldie was a baby in long clothes, had entered his dusty and cobwebbed repositories, and was seeking through their stone shelves for some fine old crusted port of a peculiar vintage, kept alone for the use of his master and himself, when the cry of Allan and some other strange sounds reached his ears, as he thought, and seriously startled him.

We say he thought, for the recess of his wine binns was an unlikely place to hear any other sound than that made by a scared rat.

It was now the dead, dull silence of midnight, when the sounds that are unknown amid the buzz of mid-day life are heard, and seem so oddly, so preternaturally loud and strange—a crack in a door panel or wainscot, the tap of a moth against the window-panes, distant noises that come we know not how or from what on the still damp air.

In a country house at night there is usually a solemn stillness that is painful and oppressive to the wakeful; and it was amidst this silence, the cry—for a human cry it was—reached the butler's startled ear.

But whence had it come? Out of the stone wall, or from the ground beneath, or from the throat of a raven in one of the great chimneys of the old house?

'Impossible!' thought Tappleton; 'it was the voice of a man—or a ghost.'

At the latter idea he closed the wine-binn door, and retired with precipitation to his cosy room, and thought the matter over as he stirred and sipped his hot whisky toddy, but feeling ever and anon that wild throbbing of the heart, and 'that electric chill and rising of the hair which accompanies supernatural panic.'

The old man had a most uncomfortable feeling about the voice he had heard, and its strangely muffled sound seemed to come in fancy to his ear again and again; and now he, not unnaturally, began to associate it with the mysterious disappearance of Allan, the Master.

With earliest dawn he betook himself to his wine cellar again, and felt that he was a bolder man in daylight than in the gloom of midnight; but 'most men are,' says Charles Dickens; yet when an unmistakable moan or two reached his ears, his fear of the supernatural so nearly gained the ascendancy that he was about to take to flight again.

However he paused, while his old heart beat painfully, and began to think of what adjoined his cellars, and at once there flashed upon his memory the locality of the horrible old vault; for the butler knew all the 'outs and ins' of Dundargue as well as if he had built it.

In the course of modern alterations and repairs a portion of the originally enormous wall of the vault had been thinned and cut away. There were crannies in the masonry, and it was through these the voice of the imprisoned had reached the butler during his casual visit to his cellar.

'Some one is there. Good Heavens! if it should be the Master—the Master after a'!' exclaimed Tappleton; and, quick as his old legs could carry him, he rushed up stairs, through the picture-gallery, along the arched corridor, and reached at last the oak trap-door; but when he saw it, with its great iron hasp over the rusted staple, hope died away, and his soul sank within him.

Loth to linger in a place where, as we have stated, superstition believed that those who did so, had a creeping sense of having near them shadowy forms and intangible presences, he was on the point of turning away, when, controlling his silly fears, he thought he might as well pursue his investigations further.

He raised the trap-door, and almost immediately a voice ascended to his ear from the darkness below. He peered down, but could see nothing.

'Wha is there—wha spoke?' asked the butler.

'I—I, the Master,' replied the weak voice of Allan Graham.

'You, sir—heaven be gude tae us! You sir! hoo in God's name cam' ye to be doon there?' cried Tappleton, in mingled joy, horror, and great perplexity.

'Summon help—there's a good old fellow; get me out, and then you will know all—quick, Tappleton, or—or I shall not last much longer,' replied Allan, faintly, and at intervals, in a voice so low that his last words seemed to die away, while Tappleton rushed off as fast as his years would permit, to seek Lord Aberfeldie and alarm the whole household, which he did very effectually by a sudden and furious application to the great house-bell, causing a very general idea of fire, and bringing all from their rooms in various kinds of *déshabille* at that early hour of the morning.

'The Master's found—the Master's found!' he kept shouting on every hand.

'Where—where?' asked twenty voices.

'Ay, ye may weel ask *whar*,' was the tantalizing response.

In the breast of Lord Aberfeldie and all his household incredulity at first, and then profound astonishment, reigned for a time on the butler making himself understood, and all hastened to the scene of his discovery.

'The Master—the Master down there,' muttered the servants, looking inquiringly in each other's faces. 'How came such a thing to pass?'

They jostled and impeded each other; but Lord Aberfeldie's authority and soldier-like promptitude soon defined a line of action.

'Lights—lights and ropes; look alive, men!' he exclaimed.

These requisites were soon brought.

'Lower away—take courage—we'll soon have you out,' exclaimed his father. 'Tie the ropes tightly round you.'

Allan, in a faint voice, made them aware that this was impossible, as his left arm was broken, tidings which added commiseration and grief to the blank amazement of Olive, Eveline, and his mother.

'Who will go down?' asked Lord Aberfeldie, looking around him.

'I—and I—and I!'

Every man in the house was ready to descend, but Angus Glas, the active young deerstalker, slid down the rope with a lanthorn in his hand, followed by the prayer of Olive, who would not be kept back, her eyes wild, her now pale lips apart, her sweet face blanched, and a strange stiffness in all her usually lithe limbs.

Pale as death, his face plastered with dried blood—blood that had flowed from a contusion in his head—livid and helpless, his left arm hanging limp as an empty sleeve by his side, his eyes half closed, as if unable to endure the glare of the day after being so long in the dark, Allan was brought up, and, on beholding him, the exclamations of commiseration and astonishment redoubled; and yet it could be seen that he was almost past questioning, and mounted grooms were instantly despatched to summon all the medical aid of the district.

Had the butler's nocturnal visit to his binns been twenty-four hours later, Allan Graham must have perished, and his fate might never have been known in his own generation perhaps.

The whole catastrophe seemed so strange, unintelligible, unnatural, and harrowing that the nerves of Lady Aberfeldie were terribly shaken by it; so were those of her daughter and Olive, and each needed all the comfort and support the other could give.

Some wine, which he drank thirstily, first revived the patient after he was conveyed to his room.

'How in the name of heaven, Allan, came you to fall into that place?' asked his father.

'I did not fall in,' replied Allan, in a species of husky whisper.

'How then?'

'Holcroft!' was all Allan could utter, when the room seemed to swim round him and he became insensible.

Lord Aberfeldie knew not precisely what to make of the reply, but suspicion gave him a certain clue to what he thought had happened, and the same idea seemed to occur to young Angus, the gillie, who was assisting to undress his master and put him to bed, for his eyes gleamed under their shaggy brows, and he could only mutter from time to time,

'*Cead mille maloch!*'

A malediction in which Lord Aberfeldie heartily concurred.

When ultimately the Peer learned all that had transpired, the incident of the cheque he had so innocently and generously given Holcroft was completely forgotten. He felt only rage, mingled with utter stupefaction, that a man could act so basely as his recent guest had done. It was altogether out of his calculation and experience of human life in every way.

'But what is to be done now—to search out and punish this malignant scoundrel?' he exclaimed; while Lady Aberfeldie, all her motherly feelings outraged, was for raising fire and sword, and letting loose all the terrors of the law on Holcroft's head.

Lord Aberfeldie, however, after a time thought differently. He had a horror of publicity, of newspaper gossip and scandals, of making his honoured and ancestral home and the affairs of his family a *point d'appui*, as he said, for such things—a world's wonder, even for a time; and thus he declined to attempt to punish Holcroft for an outrage none had seen him commit.

He would leave that to the course of events, and to Time, the avenger.

More than all, the name of Olive Raymond might crop up in the unseemly matter.

'His father was a brave, good fellow, and my dearest friend!' said Lord Aberfeldie sadly; 'how comes his son to be such an utter villain? He has drawn his evil tendencies from some past generation; it is said that such a kind of poison is at times transmitted in the blood, and that no human being can truly value the resistance of sin or folly.'

But Lady Aberfeldie was stormy, and declined to be pacified.

'We have the future to think of,' said her husband again; 'evil tongues to guard against for the sake of Olive, our whole family, and my old comrade the General, who is now in his grave—the father of that foul ingrate.'

Thus it was that no mention of the affair was made by the daily prints, to the surprise, certainly, and perhaps the relief, of Holcroft's mind.

'Say no more on this subject, Eveline,' said Lord Aberfeldie, as he sought to soothe his wife. 'Gladly would I forget that we had ever sheltered at Dundargue a guest so degrading in character; gladly would I forget as soon as possible—if it be possible—the hours of intense suffering we have undergone, more than all that Allan must have undergone in that horrible place, and yet under his own roof!'

Many a silent and reproachful tear Olive shed in secret, as she knew, in the recent past time, how much her pride, petulance, and suspicion had done to further jealousy and resentment in the mind of Holcroft against her cousin; and she felt that too probably she had caused all this.

But Holcroft was a bankrupt and a blackleg now, and never more, at London or anywhere else, she thought, could he cross *her* path again. Till now she never believed that the world could contain a man so utterly unprincipled, so thoroughly base!

The household servants supposed that the Master had fallen into that gruesome vault by accident, and they were allowed to adopt the idea.

'But who closed the trap and dropped the hasp over the staple?' thought old Tappleton; yet eventually he allowed himself to be talked into the idea that he had made a mistake in that matter.

Allan lay long ill and delirious after all he had undergone; but when it was announced that he was past danger, great was the rejoicing of all the servants and the household at Dundargue, for all loved the Master well, and were faithfully attached to the family by ties of residence and clanship, even in this Victorian age. 'The devoted loyalty of the clansmen to their chiefs existed undiminished for generations after the system of clan government was abolished in 1746,' said the *Standard* newspaper recently; 'and it would be wholly erroneous to contend, *even now*, that the peculiar affection between the people and their chief, altogether different in nature and degree from any relationship known in a Saxon community, has died away.'

But the family of Aberfeldie had not seen the last of Mr. Hawke Holcroft.

CHAPTER VII.

LOVERS.

The early days of the spring subsequent to the events we have narrated, found the Aberfeldie family located at Maviswood, a handsome modern villa to the west of Edinburgh, whither they had removed from Dundargue, that Allan, on whom a kind of protracted illness had fallen, might avail himself of the great medical skill which is always to be found in the Scottish Metropolis.

By what means Allan was discovered and got out of the vault into which he had been flung, and, as Hawke Holcroft hoped, was entombed for ever, the latter never knew, from the plan adopted by the family, but the public prints had informed him more than once, that 'the Master of Aberfeldie had met with an accident—a fall—from the effects of which he was slowly recovering; wounds received when on service with the Black Watch retarding his progress to health.'

Evan Cameron, Carslogie, and others of the regiment, then in the Castle of Edinburgh, heard of Allan's affair or illness in a vague way, as Lord Aberfeldie shrunk from all gossip, publicity and surmise; and the first-named learned that Eveline's marriage had been delayed in consequence of that illness, chiefly through a letter written to him by Olive, at Allan's request.

So the early days of spring were passing on, and no particular change had taken place in the relative positions of our characters since we last saw them at Dundargue.

Eveline was alone one afternoon in a room at Maviswood—a room of vast proportions. The ceiling was divided into deep panels of oak colour; a dado of dead gold tint was carried round the walls to within eight feet of the cornice, and the chairs and ottomans were upholstered in blue maroquin leather, studded with elaborate gilt nails. The hangings were blue, with yellow borders, lining and tassels; great china bowls, full of conservatory flowers, stood on ornate tables and pedestals, within the recess of a great triple bay window, beyond which spread away southward the lovely landscape that is bounded by the Pentlands.

Spring is a lovely and joyous season everywhere, but nowhere is it lovelier than in the fertile Lothians; and nowhere may the eye rest upon a more varied and beautiful landscape than that which spreads from the southern slope of Corstorphine's wooded crags to the base of the green and undulating Pentlands, the highest summits of which range from sixteen hundred to nearly nineteen hundred feet.

There are corn-fields teeming with fertility, rows of stately trees, pretty cottages, stately white manor houses, and cosy farms embosomed among old woods and orchards; the picturesque rocks of wooded Craiglockhart, wherein the kites and kestrels build their nests; the rich alluvial land, where for ages a great loch once spread its waters; the quaint old village church, on the spire of which the red sunset loves to linger; and westward the Queen of the North, in all the glory of castled rock, and hill and crag, spire, tower, and countless terraces; and on all of these the wistful eyes of Eveline Grahame were wandering dreamily.

A golden glory was cast along the eastern slopes, the fleecy clouds were every moment assuming new forms and lovelier colours; the woods were budding forth; the Leith and its tiny tributaries were brawling along as if their waters had no time to toy with the brown pebbles. Seated, at times, sideways on their horses, the happy ploughboys were already going home from their labours. The early-yeaned lambs were frisking about the ewes, and cloud and sunshine seemed to chase each other over the tender grass, where the wild white gowan was opening its petals, and old folks were remembering that 'a peck o' March dust was worth the ransom o' a king.'

Of late, Eveline's bursts of girlish merriment had been few and far between. She was fretful—unusually so for a girl who by nature was so sweet and gentle, and at the mere mention of the name of Sir Paget—to whom she felt herself doomed, as it were, or allotted—she became more fretful, silent, and abstracted.

She shrank from smiling people, turned her back upon inquisitive ones, and often was found to answer briefly and beside the point.

In short, the pretty Eveline's heart or mind was quite unhinged.

The tenth day of her residence at Maviswood was creeping slowly on, and she was pondering, full of thought, alone in that stately room, when a servant startled her by announcing and ushering in 'Mr. Evan Cameron,' and, though her mind was full of him—of the evening of the carpet-dance at Dundargue, and the hour of joy in the half-lit corridor, a kind of gasp escaped her as she rose from her seat to receive him.

But why should he not call, reason suggested to her.

The Grahams had been for ten days, we have said, at Maviswood; and Cameron, who had been counting every hour of those ten days, and watching the villa with his field-glass from his quarters in the distant castle, had now ventured to make an afternoon walk, and found, beyond his hopes, that Eveline was alone.

Allan and Olive were out together in a pony-phaeton; Lord and Lady Aberfeldie were he cared not where; anyway, they were absent too.

Olive, feeling that she was in some way responsible, by her past thoughtlessness, petulance, and flirting with the daring and unworthy Holcroft, for much that had befallen Allan, now 'waited on him hand and foot,' as the old nurse Nannie phrased it. She was with him from hour to hour, and, though their marriage was delayed, how happy they seemed to be!

Fearing interruption as before, Cameron, too tender and true not to be a timid lover, found a difficulty just then in taking up the thread of the old story, and they stood in the bay-window talking commonplaces, while heart was speaking to heart and eye to eye. But 'what is speaking or hearing when heart wells into heart?'

Cameron heard all she chose then to tell him about Allan's 'accident,' the bewilderment and alarm of the family, and so forth. Many friends were spoken of, but Sir Paget was of course referred to by neither.

Eveline, though so young, had the frank and perfect air of repose in her manner that came of gentle breeding, and made her seem older than she was, but gave an assurance that whatever she said, or whatever she did, was said and done in the right way. Without coquetry, her manner was full of simple fascination; but it was undeniably nervous now, for she read by Cameron's softened voice, and in his brightening eye, the clear necessity for something else than common-place talk, when he discovered by a casual remark that Lord and Lady Aberfeldie were not in the house.

Eveline felt that she had given herself to Evan, and that the tenor of their interview in the corridor amounted tacitly to an engagement.

An engagement! But to what end? It all seemed but a dream, a delicious dream, of which there was nothing to remind her, not even a ring, a lock of hair, or the tiniest note.

Unlike Cameron, Eveline, while loving him dearly, had, singular to say, no thought of marriage with him in the ordinary sense of the word; for, hemmed round as she was, and destined as she was, the idea was a hopeless one, judged from her parents' point of view. She only felt, poor girl, that she loved, and was full of sad joy—if we may use the paradox—in the belief that she was truly loved in return.

'How silent you have become,' she said, in a low tone, after a nervous pause.

'I know not what to say; but love has no need of words, Eveline, nor needs he many at any time,' he replied, drawing closer to her. Then he took a conservatory rose from a vase and exclaimed, 'Eveline darling, you love me well and truly, don't you?'

'Well and truly, you know, dear Evan,' she replied, as his arm went round her, and her head dropped on his shoulder. 'What need to ask me?' she whispered, in a breathless voice.

'Because I cannot hear the beloved assurance too often.' He kissed her tenderly, we cannot say how many times, nor would it matter, while she lay passive in his arms, and then he said, 'Shall we try our fate with this rose?'

'How?'

'By plucking it, leaf by leaf, saying each time "Lucky, Unlucky," till the last leaf comes.'

'Something *à la Marguerite*.'

'Yes.'

'No, decidedly no, dearest Evan.'

'You are superstitious. Well, so am I.'

'Thus an omen would only torment us, and surely we have enough—enough——' Tears choked her voice, and she could only add, 'Trust, dearest Evan, trust.'

'In what, my darling?'

'The great goodness of God.'

The spell of a great love was on both. Their lips met in a long and silent kiss, and the rose fell at their feet between them.

A sound roused them—nay, startled them. They had only time to separate and affect a sudden interest in the artistic effects produced by light and shadow on the landscape, when Lord and Lady Aberfeldie entered the room together, a pretty palpable cloud of annoyance resting on the brows of both as they politely, but far from warmly, greeted the visitor.

The peer, who had evidently been out riding, appeared in a black morning coat and white cords, whip in hand, and the lady, who had been in the grounds, wore her garden hat and shawl. She had seen a visitor ride up to the door from a distant part of the lawn, and had hurried home, her heart foreboding truly who that visitor was.

And now, while their hearts were vibrating with tenderness, and with their lips yet tremulously sensible of the sweetness of kisses—the first kisses of a new and early love—they had to talk enforced commonplace—or, at least, Evan did so, while Eveline remained silent—of the news of the day, the expected plans of the ministry, the probable despatch of a fleet to Egyptian waters, of the chances of an army following it, of Arabi Pasha and the Khedive, the plot formed by the Circassian officers, and so forth, till it was time for the lingering Cameron to resume his hat and depart at last.

Cameron tried to ignore that which, under other and more prosperous circumstances, would have galled and roused his haughty Highland spirit—Lord Aberfeldie's coldness of manner when he spoke even of the regiment, and how certainly it would go to the East, 'as the Black Watch, thank God, was always in everything, and always with honour,' while Evan's eyes irresistibly wandered to the face of Eveline, and memory went back to the twilighted corridor at Dundargue.

But so did the memory of my Lord Aberfeldie.

The peer must have undergone a good deal of training or "drilling" lately at the hands of Lady Aberfeldie before he could have brought himself to behave so coldly to one he really liked so well as young Stratherroch, and one of the Black Watch especially; but then, perhaps, he was just a little soured by the sequel to the hospitality and kindness accorded to "the son of his old friend," which son had contrived by skilful lettering and figuring to add the sum of eighty pounds to his cheque.

As he bade them adieu Stratherroch observed that Lord Aberfeldie did not ask him to call again at Maviswood, and keenly did he feel the omission and all it implied, and with it came the conviction that he must call no more!

Slowly he rode back to his quarters full of alternately exultant and bitter thoughts—exultant that Eveline loved him and would never cease to love him, but bitter ones as he asked himself, to what end!

If poor Cameron had vague and lingering hopes to which he clung (and doubtless he had)—hopes when seeing Eveline, of proposing or hinting of meeting elsewhere in the future—they were doomed to blight, for no such bore fruition; and they had now parted, and her father and mother thought they should part, as mere friends, who might meet casually in society, but at all events had better *not* meet again.

And Cameron feared that, so far as monetary matters stood with him, his friend Allan might endorse the same view of the situation.

'Stratherroch is a gentleman by birth and position, but poor, miserably poor,' said Lady Aberfeldie, after he had gone; 'so was that precious Mr. Holcroft, and when a declension takes place in tone, manner, and habits, as in his instance, we never know where it may end,' she added pointedly to Eveline.

'How can you speak of the two men in the same sentence!' exclaimed the peer, with an asperity for which his daughter thanked him in her aching heart.

At anytime when Eveline looked south-eastward from Maviswood she could see the Castle of Edinburgh, and the towering mass of the western barrack, with all its windows shining in the sun, and she always did so with tenderest interest, as she knew that *he* was there; but, natheless, her experience of at least one London season, there was much of the guileless child and mere girl in Eveline still, and she was so sweet and soft, so pliable, and so impressed with her mother's will and her father's authority, that—that how could Evan Cameron tell what pressure might be brought to bear upon her, to make her seem to transfer the allegiance of her heart to another—even to the wealthy old English baronet, Sir Paget Puddicombe?

Alas! there was to be, in time, a pressure that none could then foresee.

CHAPTER VIII.

AT MAVISWOOD.

The reports which Mr. Hawke Holcroft—spinning out his precarious existence by skill with the billiard cue, cards, and the betting ring—heard concerning the health of his intended victim, one whom he still absurdly and grotesquely deemed his successful rival, were undoubtedly true.

With all his natural strength. Allan Graham recovered but slowly from all he had undergone, and the many hours he had lingered in that vault with his fractured limb unset, together with the effect of certain sabre wounds received when he served in India, retarded his progress to restoration; but amid his protracted convalescence how sweet it was, as the pleasant days of sunny spring stole on at Maviswood, to have the society, the hourly care and attendance of Olive, in whom he was always, he thought, discovering some new charm of mind or grace of manner, with much soft tenderness of heart and hand.

Thus, twice—once in India and again at home—rescued, as it were, from the verge of death, he had learned the sweetness of life, and that, whatever its sufferings and sorrows may be, what a priceless gift it is—a reflection that never occurred to him when going under fire, or leading a line of Highlanders in their headlong charge.

Lady Aberfeldie was content and happy; Evan Cameron seemed now a banished man; even Allan never spoke of him, and the progress of matters between the cousins proved all she could desire.

'Nothing could be more fortunate, dearest Olive, than the attachment which now subsists between you and Allan; it fulfils all your father's fondest wishes,' said she, as she met them one day in the garden, slowly promenading between the flowerbeds, Allan leaning, or affecting to do so, on the soft, round arm of Olive.

'Yes, mother dear—I agree with you, and also with Peter Simple,' replied Allan, smiling.

'In what?'

'That the life of a man seems to consist of getting into scrapes, and then getting out of them again.'

'And you forget now that I ever teased and tormented you so, my poor Allan,' said Olive, patting his rather pale cheek with her pinky palm.

'Of course I do, darling. I am not much of a philosopher, but Balzac is right in his view of human life—that it would be intolerable without a vast amount of forgetting.'

'And forgiving, too, he might have added,' said Olive, as she tendered her lips playfully and poutingly for a kiss, which he was not slow in according.

Poor Eveline, as she watched this happy pair daily under her eyes, sighed with natural and irrepressible envy; she thought of her own love for Evan Cameron—secret, ignored, and so liable to excite maternal scorn and bitterness, with paternal reprehension, when it came on the *tapis*; while even Allan, at all times so loving and so brotherly, amid the great selfishness or absorption of his own passion, seemed, as she thought, to have withdrawn his sympathy from her now.

One circumstance she deemed most fortunate—Parliament was sitting, and Sir Paget Puddicombe was in London.

It would seem, then, that between the botheration of Ireland and the interests of Egypt the affairs of Slough-cum-Sloggit—monetary, municipal, and commercial—were as likely to be forgotten and ignored as if that quiet borough had actually been an integral part of Scotland—a state of matters not to be tolerated. So Sir Paget was in his place at Westminster, jerking his head and puffing out his chest more than ever, and Eveline was freed for a time from his presence, and the would-be lover-like regard of his suspicious and keenly-critical old eyes.

And she knew not that almost daily, the moment that he was free from duty or parade was over, Evan, drawn by an irrepressible craving and desire to be near her—to see the roof under which she dwelt, the windows through which she might be looking, the trees under which she might be walking, was always hovering in the vicinity of Maviswood; while, by a strange fatality, she, filled by a similar desire, might be riding with her father, or driving with her mother, through stately George Street, along the magnificent terrace of Princes Street, and other great thoroughfares, looking eagerly, but in vain, for a chance glimpse of him, and perhaps a bow—a mere bow, and nothing more.

Circumstanced as they were, what more could she look for?

Twice only, and at long intervals, did she see Evan, and on each occasion how wildly did her loving heart beat as she detected his well-known figure; but he saw not her, as she rode slowly on by her father's side, who, if he saw Evan on the first occasion, steadily ignored the fact, and stared up at the Castle ramparts, where the sentinels of the Black Watch trod slowly to and fro.

Certainly Evan did not see her. He was on the garden side of Princes Street the wooded walk which somewhat resembles a continental boulevard—in close conversation with a young lady, who seemed to listen to all he was saying with great *empressement.*

The second time she saw him was after an interval of some days, in the same place, at the same hour, and with the same fair companion, to whom her father—thinking, no doubt, to utilise the circumstance—drew her attention somewhat pointedly.

'Cameron *again*!' said he; 'our friend seems to find other attractions in the gardens than trees or spring flowers.'

Eveline's heart beat painfully, and the second episode gave her occasion for much and rather harassing thought. Her father, by this remark, showed that he had observed Evan before; but who was the latter's companion?

Eveline blushed violently up to where the brim of her smart riding-hat pressed her bright brown hair upon her brow, and down to where a stiff and snow-white linen collar encircled her slender white neck; then she grew very pale with constrained emotion, which, fortunately, her father did not detect.

She did not speak, but pretended to smile, with an effort of self-mastery, while a lump seemed to rise in her slender throat; for though the circumstance of Evan, who was debarred from coming to see her, being seen there again with the same young lady might be a casualty, a trivial coincidence, and quite explainable, her pride was piqued and her affection wounded.

Still more were they piqued and wounded when, some days after, as she was seated in the carriage at the door of a shop in which Lady Aberfeldie was giving some orders, she saw this girl loitering in the same spot, looking anxiously around her, as if waiting for some one who did not come, and whom Eveline's heart foreboded could only be Evan Cameron!

She snatched from the carriage-basket or reticule a lorgnette, through which she could see that the girl was more than pretty, very pale, and though plainly yet fashionably dressed, with an undoubtedly ladylike air and bearing.

If he was Evan she waited for, he did not keep his appointment, for, after a time, the stranger turned sadly, lingeringly away, and disappeared.

A dancing-man, a popular young fellow like Evan Cameron, in one of the most popular of Scottish regiments, could not fail to have many lady friends in Edinburgh; but to have been seen twice in the same place, with the same girl, at the same time, and apparently expected there a *third* time, was a little peculiar, and apt to cause Eveline to speculate upon it unpleasantly.

Was this companionship a matter of daily occurrence? Or was he, amid the enforced separation from herself, beginning to replace her image by another already—already?

The tenderness of their last meeting, in the bay-window at Maviswood, seemed to preclude this cruel idea, and to the hope that tenderness inspired, she clung most lovingly; thus, as yet, she did not speak of the matter to her cousin Olive, who—full of her own love-affair and her new-found happiness—might not have sympathised with her as once she would have done; and, to add to her trouble, in a little time she would have her old admirer beside her again, as the member for Slough-cum-Sloggit was making arrangements to pair off with another, and would soon be able to leave London.

However, some happiness was in store for her still.

Cameron, to do him justice, spent too much of his spare time in hovering about the vicinity of Maviswood not to be rewarded. Thus, one clear, bright afternoon, in a lovely and lonely green lane, where the holly hedges grew close and darkly, where the wood violets spread their velvet leaves on the sunny banks, and where the mavis and merle sang, they suddenly met each other, as he came walking slowly along on foot, leading his horse by the bridle, which was flung over his arm.

His heart was so full of her that, when he met her suddenly face to face thus, he scarcely evinced surprise, while tremulously she put both her hands into his.

'Evan!'

'My darling—at last—at last!'

No eye was upon them there as his arms went round her, and in the great joy of seeing him, of meeting him thus, the two occasions on which she had seen him with another, promenading slowly under the trees in Princes Street, were forgotten and committed to oblivion; though ere long they were to be roughly brought to her memory.

'Oh, Evan—such long looked-for—such unexpected joy!' she exclaimed, as hand in hand they gazed into each other's eyes.

'Joy indeed, my own one. I had begun to fear we might never meet again; and I shall not leave you now but with the assurance that we shall meet as often as we can till—till——'

'When, Evan?'

'The regiment marches—marches for the East, as it is sure to do before long. Eveline, you must be out in the garden, in the grounds often; can I not meet you there or here again?'

She shook her head sadly, and looked at him lovingly and imploringly.

'The meetings in secret—without permission—would be wrong, Evan,' said she.

'Permission—who will give it? Whom—what have we to consult but our own hearts?' he continued, passionately. 'We may have but little time—less than we reckon on now—for the interchange of love and joy, my dear one; and meet me you shall—you *must*,' he added, as he folded her to his breast and covered her sweet passive face with kisses, while something of hostility and defiance at her whole family and at Sir Paget welled up in his heart. 'You will meet me again?' he urged.

'Yes,' she replied, in a scarcely audible whisper.

It could be no sin, no crime—if an error—to meet one who loved her so well as Evan did, and whom she loved so dearly too. It could not harm her elderly adorer, from whose image just then she shrank with intense loathing; and, if it was a wrong against her parents, surely they were in error to coerce her, she thought.

On the other hand, the temptation was great; the joy of meeting Evan would end sadly and bitterly when, as he said, the regiment departed, and after that they might never see each other more!

'Stolen waters are sweet, and bread eaten in secret is pleasant,' say the Scriptures; and not less sweet and pleasant were the interviews that might be stolen thus in a green and lonely lane.

'God help me and direct me!' thought the girl, as she nestled her face in Cameron's neck, and, yielding to the natural impulses of her own heart, promised to meet him again and again, when time and opportunity served; and they did so in the lane between the holly hedges, by the rural woodland road that deep between the hills, leads to Ravelston Quarry and haunted Craigcrook; and at times near the old church, where the buried Forresters lie under their altar tombs with shield on arm and sword at side; and as the days went on each meeting—as it seemed to take place without suspicion or discovery—served to cement their hearts together more and more.

But once, when Evan was riding home in the dusk in the vicinity of Maviswood, he passed a wayfarer afoot, in whose face he thought he recognised—nay, was certain he saw—the features of Holcroft.

'Holcroft!' thought Evan; 'a man to guard against, by Jove. What can *he* be about in this neighbourhood—what but mischief?'

He wheeled his horse round, but the man he had seen, had stepped over a stile and disappeared.

CHAPTER IX.

'ALICE!'

My Lady Aberfeldie was all unconscious of the little romance that had been going on for some weeks past in the green lanes and wooded paths near Maviswood; while Eveline seemed now but to live for the purpose of meeting Evan Cameron, and her loving heart and busy little head were full of cunning schemes and contrivances to escape detection and achieve their meetings, which now seemed to make the whole sense of her existence; and when not with Evan, or if they failed (which was seldom) to see each other, even for a few minutes, her manner became abstracted and triste.

But a rude awakening from her joyous dreams was at hand, and certain past events that seemed trivial in themselves were doomed to be recalled to her with a new and terrible significance!

They had one more than usually tender meeting and tender parting, because Sir Paget Puddicombe—the *bête noir*, the bugbear of both—was certainly coming to Maviswood, and Eveline was weeping bitterly.

'Take courage—take courage, my darling,' said Evan, as he kissed the tears from her eyes and strained her to his breast before he leaped on his horse; 'for my sake and your own have strength to resist, and all may yet be well—for my sake and your own, dearest Alice,' he added, with quivering lips, and was gone.

'*Alice!*'

Another's name uttered by his lips involuntarily while his heart seemed to be teeming with tenderness for herself—uttered in that moment of supreme sorrow, passion, and endearment—escaped him mechanically, as it were, yet too evidently by use and wont!

What did it mean—what could it mean, but one thing?

Her heart stood still for a moment and then beat wildly; she did not hear the noise of his horse's hoofs dying away in the distance, nor did she see his lessening figure, for the powers of hearing and of vision seemed to fail her.

She had received a cruel and terrible shock. Had she heard aright, or was it all a delusion of her ear, yet she repeated to herself with pallid face and quivering lips the word 'Alice!' while memory flashed back to the girl she had seen thrice—twice with Evan, and once evidently waiting for him at what seemed their trysting-place.

She remembered that the second time she had seen them they were walking silently together—full of their own thoughts apparently—and making no effort to entertain each other, and she had read that it is only 'the nearest and dearest' of kinships—the closest and sweetest of human intimacies that could explain such "wordless proximity." Strangers, acquaintances, when thrown together *must* politely talk; brother and sister, husband and wife, may be confidently, blessedly silent!'

She remembered now, with ready suspicion, that, when she and Evan first met suddenly afterwards, he scarcely evinced surprise. We have said that it was because his heart was full of her image, but this idea, this hope, did not occur to Eveline then—her mind was a chaos.

How she got through the remainder of that day she never knew; she had but one wish: to shun her mother's eye. To seclude herself in her own room would attract attention; thus she remained in the drawing-room and affected to read. She opened a book at the page and point where she had last left off.

Alas! it was beyond the power of books to soothe or win her from herself now. The Lethean power of the novelist had departed, and her whole mind seemed out of tune.

She threw aside the volume and took up another, but a cry escaped her as it fell from her hands. It was Bulwer's 'Alice, or the Mysteries;' the name seemed to enter her heart like a knife, and she rushed away to her room.

The dressing-bell for dinner, when it rang, found her very pale, and wrestling, as it were, with a strange and unusual pain that was eating its way into her heart.

She bathed her face again and again, but failed to hide the dark shadows under her eyes or the inflammation of their delicate lids.

And at dinner-time that evening an additional stab was given to her in the most casual and unexpected way. Her father had brought from his club to Maviswood Carslogie of the Black Watch, a heedless and thoughtless young fellow, of whom she overheard Allan making some inquiries concerning Cameron of Stratherroch.

'Oh, Strath is jolly as a sandboy,' replied Carslogie, 'but he has some mysterious affair of the heart on just now.'

'How?'

'In the usual way. There is a pretty girl he goes about with to all public places, but introduces to no one. She is without a chaperone, and no one knows whether she is maid, wife, or widow; funny, by Jove, isn't it?'

Carslogie said this in a low voice to Allan, yet not so low but that it reached the ears of Eveline, who had some difficulty in concealing her agitation.

With instinctive tenderness Allan glanced at his sister and skilfully changed the subject to the then invariable topic of Arabi Pasha and 'the coming row in Egypt.'

Times there were when she had thought that she would condescend to go once again to their trysting-place, and seek an explanation; but now, after what Carslogie had said, wild horses should not drag her there!

She would never upbraid Evan with his baseness, never more would she go there; she would simply tear his image out of her heart, and let the matter end. But this was easier to say than to achieve.

Her soul seemed to have become numbed within her—frozen, if we may use such terms.

Even in the matter of Sir Paget, she was conscious now of feeling neither repugnance nor ridicule, though she felt a little repentance at her opposition to the wishes of her father and mother, and for the duplicity of which she had been guilty towards them in her love for an unworthy object, and meeting him in secret, as if she had been a sewing-girl or waiting-maid, and not the daughter of a peer, and putting herself, perhaps, in an equivocal position.

She confided in Olive; otherwise her heart, she thought, would burst.

'The heart is said to be "deceitful above all things, and desperately wicked,"' said Olive, 'but I must confess that this affair passes my comprehension. He cannot be in love with *two* at once; yet I have read of such things. Forget him; you must do that—at least. You endure too much, Eveline; you believed in him too much, and, I fear, hoped too much. Even friendship has its limits; how much more so love.'

'And but yesterday I was so happy—happy in a love the end of which I could not foresee!' wailed poor Eveline, on her cousin's bosom.

What was she like, this Alice? Her rival—oh, disgrace! Fair or dark—she remembered that she was pale and pretty. But what did it matter, thought the now crushed girl, as she tossed feverishly on her pillow in the gloom and solitude of the night, when even our thoughts seem to assume distinct outlines that become sharp and vivid.

Night had passed—a new day dawned, and how far, far off seemed yesterday! The sun had risen in his glory; the blackbirds were singing in the dew-laden shrubberies of Maviswood; and the pale mists were clearing off Torduff and Kirkyetton Craig, the highest summits of the lovely Pentlands.

It was late ere Eveline had wept herself to sleep; but to her it seemed as if she had not slept at all. Thus it was proportionately late when she awoke heavily to the morning of a new day.

She had given her whole soul with joy to her hopeless love for Evan—hopeless, but pure—though any happy end to it she could not foresee; but this was a bitter collapse she did not anticipate, and now her 'occupation was gone.'

Was she the same Eveline Graham who but yesterday morning shook off sleep so lightly, and rose fresh, strong, and full of hope, with the conviction that her secret lover was true to her and to this hopeless passion?

Her affectionate heart was crushed; her self-esteem was in the dust; her proud head lay low indeed; and for the first time in her young life she had learned what it is to be cut to the soul—to be completely humbled.

And Alice—who and what was *she*?

'And oh, Olive, how am I to meet mamma?' was the first exclamation after they had got rid of Mademoiselle Clairette.

She knew she would have to join in the conversation of the breakfast-table, when all her vigilance would be requisite to prevent her from pit-falls of suspicious silence or confusion of manner, with the helpless air and uncertain voice of one who seeks to conceal a new and hitherto unknown sorrow: and to undergo, with her sad, white, humiliated face, her mother's critical and observant eyes.

If, in desperation, she did not act a part, that watchful mother would be sure to detect a change, and that there was something wrong.

Eveline knew well that she would soon detect every flicker of her eyelashes, every tremor of the heavy white lids, that would droop in spite of her now; but luckily Lady Aberfeldie was busy in her boudoir with the housekeeper and Mr. Tappleton, the butler, giving orders; for Sir Paget Puddicombe would arrive ere long!

Carslogie had gone back to Edinburgh, of course, last night. He would be with Evan Cameron this morning on parade and so forth; would the latter question him about his visit to Maviswood, about *her* perhaps? But what did it matter now whether he did so or did not? Nothing—less than nothing!

How long the hours seemed now when they were empty—*quite* empty of all but bitterness.

Meanwhile days passed on, and Cameron came, as was his wont, to the usual places of meeting, but Eveline was never there.

What had happened—how was she detained? Had an illness come upon her? His mind was a prey to the keenest anxiety, which he was without the means of allaying. He could not write to ask for any explanation, neither could he call at Maviswood after the somewhat studied coldness of his last reception there by her father and mother.

At each place and spot where so lately they had met and wandered, the thoughts that found utterance there, and many a tender caress came potently and poignantly back to memory now. Where was she, what doing, how engaged and with whom—in sickness or in health?—he asked of himself with endless iteration.

Trivialities are often associated with the greatest eventualities in our lives. Thus long in the memory of Evan would his last visit to one of these beloved spots be associated with the shrill notes of a mavis perched upon the topmost bough of a tree.

Ignorant as yet of what he himself had done, ignorant also of the mischief his friend Carslogie had unintentionally done him by retailing some mess-room gossip, in the vagueness of his thoughts and ideas of the whole situation, which we shall ere-long unravel, Cameron was inclined to attribute the total cessation of Eveline's meetings with him to some mysterious influence of Hawke Holcroft—if Holcroft it was whom he saw in the dusk.

From Carslogie he learned that 'she was looking well and jolly,' as he phrased it. When Allan rejoined he would hear more of her, he hoped; but Allan's sick leave was protracted from time to time, and none seemed to know *when* he would be with the regiment again.

Once these parted lovers saw each other but for a moment only!

Accompanied by a groom, Eveline rode at a canter past him on a lonely part of the road near Maviswood, her eyes full of unshed tears, her face pale with resentment, and her veil in her teeth.

Past him, as if he was a stranger!

'Why stop to speak or expect an explanation?' thought the girl. 'In this world do not actions speak louder a thousand times than words can ever do?'

She was a Graham of Dundargue, and would show him that she was not of the kind of stuff that facile Amelias or patient Griseldas are made!

Yet to pass him by thus, cost her a mighty effort, though to Eveline it seemed that there was nothing left for her now 'but to wrestle valiantly with that pain which, in the world's eye, degrades the woman who smarts under it—the pain of an unshared love.'

CHAPTER X.

'THE MYSTERIES OF UDOLPHO.'

'Young Stratherroch seems to have accepted the situation. He is much too sharp and well-bred a man not to have seen that he was—well—in the way rather,' said Lady Aberfeldie to her husband one afternoon. 'One thing is certain at least, he has ceased to visit here.'

'Dropped out of the hunt—yes,' assented the peer, as he filled and lit his briar-root. 'Poor fellow! he was—or is—undoubtedly fond of our little girl.'

'Such fondness was folly in one so poor; and now, as Sir Paget comes to-day, I do not see why we should not have the two marriages at once. I am most anxious to have all this fuss ended and done with.'

'There are several deeds to draw and so forth in the matter of Allan and Olive; and as for Eveline she has not yet consented.'

'She must do so now, I presume,' said Lady Aberfeldie, impatiently wafting aside with her white hand a cloud of smoke the peer was creating.

'Both marriages,' said he, reflectively; 'but how if the regiment goes on foreign service—and the corps expects orders of readiness daily, I understand?'

'Allan can send in his papers.'

'Impossible! You do not consider what you say.'

'He is not well enough to go abroad.'

'He is too well to remain behind; and if well enough to marry I fear that F.M. the Commander-in-Chief will deem him well enough to march.'

'Anyway it will secure Olive's fortune in the family.'

'It is secured as it is by her father's will so long as Allan is willing to consent; but as our loving daughter-in-law, there will be no necessity for the enforcement of the clause that is so grotesque. As regards Sir Paget and Eveline——'

'Leave me to manage Eveline,' said Lady Aberfeldie, bluntly and loftily.

The result of her management was soon apparent, though she knew not that circumstances, of which she was as yet unaware, were playing into her hands, and would yet more completely do so.

'Sir Paget, as you know, Eveline, will be here to-day,' said she, with an arm round her daughter's neck, 'and we—that is, your papa and I—trust, child, that you will receive him as you ought, and wear the jewels he sent you.'

Lady Aberfeldie used her softest yet firmest voice as she spoke to Eveline, but it sounded to the latter as the voice of one who was a long, long way off.

She made no immediate reply; but with her hands tightly interlaced, as if thereby she would quell emotion, seemed to be gazing down at her nicely pointed little foot that rested on a velvet fender-stool.

'Why mope here, growing pale and thin, for a thing without substance—a dream—a shadow, Eveline; you understand me?'

'A dream—a shadow, indeed, mamma!'

'You hear me, child?' said her mother.

'Yes, mamma,' replied Eveline, who seemed to shiver with cold as her mother left her, but with a long backward glance that had more of menace than entreaty in it.

'He never loved me,' Eveline was thinking. 'I have given my heart for nothing, and am now cast aside for another, like a broken toy discarded by a child. He dared to trifle with me—my father's daughter! It is clear now that he fancied, or merely pretended to be in love with me, while all the time his heart was given to—*Alice*!'

And she would have been either more or less than human, if with her just indignation there did not mingle a certain sentiment of revenge that bore her up in the part she meant to act now; though she shrank as yet from the conviction that, when esteem dies, love dies with it.

So that evening Eveline wore the suite of jewels—such jewels as Bond Street alone can furnish—and Sir Paget, as he sat by her side, jerked his little bald head about, in the exuberance of joy, and in a way that was really alarming.

Olive was looking radiantly beautiful, in a brilliant dinner costume, with Allan's Maltese suite of diamonds and pearls sparkling on her neck and arms, which Lady Aberfeldie had urged her to don in honour of Sir Paget, and in defiance of a *moue* and pitiful glance of Eveline, who had no small difficulty in acquitting herself at dinner in her new role of *fiancée*, but nearly broke down when she heard Sir Paget raise his voice and say to her father something that he was not sorry he might say with a clear conscience, and as a matter-of-fact.

'Oh, by the way, Aberfeldie, when I arrived at the rail way-station this morning I witnessed a very tender leave-taking between a young friend of yours and a most charming girl—gad, the fellow has taste—a girl whom he was seeing off, to London, I presume, by the Flying Scotsman, it was quite pathetic, by Jove!'

'A young friend of ours—who do you mean, Sir Paget?' asked Lady Aberfeldie.

'Cameron, of the Black Watch, whom I had the pleasure of meeting at Dundargue—you remember,' said Sir Paget, playing with the stem of his champagne-glass, and not daring to look at Eveline, whose white hand he saw trembling as she toyed with her grapes.

'Oh—oh—indeed—and the young lady——'

'Had "Mrs. Cameron" painted on all her luggage—great Indian overlands, some of it.'

'*Mrs. Cameron*,' repeated Lady Aberfeldie, whose aristocratic face shone in spite of herself at these tidings, while Lord Aberfeldie looked flushed and perplexed, and like Allan, who pitied his poor sister, remained silent.

This astounding intelligence was to poor Eveline as 'the last straw' to the over-laden camel; she betrayed no outward emotion, though her heart and spirit were completely broken down, for a phase of duplicity which she could never have conceived was now suddenly laid bare to her.

When, with her aunt and cousin, she retired to the drawing-room, the latter pressed her hand affectionately and caressingly, while the former, too proud or too prudent to refer to what they had just heard so greatly to her satisfaction, sat in a shady corner and slowly fanned herself in silence with a great round feather fan.

An emotion of jealous spite at young Cameron, with rivalry, passion, and ambition to possess a young, beautiful, and highly-born wife, all now inspired Sir Paget, who, to do him justice in the anecdote he had told, had told no more than the truth, and, for the happiness of Evan Cameron, we are sorry to say it.

But though now permitting herself quietly to drift with the stream of events, and to become a tool in the hands of others, it was impossible for Eveline, when with Sir Paget in the grounds, or when alone in the drawing-room, not to shrink from his now privileged caresses and attentions; thus once she shocked him by saying, as she withdrew her hands from his clasp,

'Oh, Sir Paget, do you really mean to marry a woman who does not and never can love you?'

'Do not say "never can." How can we know what the future may have for me—for *us*, my dear girl?'

'Who, indeed, save One!' sighed the girl, wearily.

'I would rather have half your heart than the whole of any other woman's,' said Sir Paget, gallantly, while recapturing her hands, and jerking out his head in turtle fashion.

'My whole heart,' thought Eveline, 'is—oh, no—was full of Evan, but can have no vacant corner for any other, especially such a man as this.'

And even while she thought this she shivered as if with cold, when in right of his new position he caressed her.

'How, with all their innate pride, papa and mamma are content to abandon me to this absurd little man Puddicombe, as they do, passes my comprehension,' said she to Olive. 'Puddicombe—such an absurd name too,' she added, with a little laugh that was hysterical; 'and what object can the splendour of his settlements be to them? They seem to ignore the fact that the Grahams of Dundargue were barons of the Scottish Parliament when the ancestors of half the British peerage were hewers of wood and drawers of water—peasantry and artisans!'

So in the bloom of her youth and beauty, the time 'when the light that surrounds us is all from within,' Eveline Graham was to become a victim at the altar after all—after all!

And Cameron seemed to have prepared the path for her, for, stunned by his too apparent duplicity, she schooled herself for the *rôle* of indifference to fate; but this was chiefly by day, for often at night she would lie where she had thrown herself, across her bed, forgetting even to undress, her tear-blotted face covered by her soft arm, and so in the morning the wondering and sympathising Clairette would find her.

June was creeping on now, with its sunny, fragrant breath; there were white and purple blossoms in the parterres of the garden; the graceful laburnums were dropping their golden petals in showers over the rosebuds and green lawns that were bordered by dark shining myrtles and deep-tinted laurels and rhododendrons.

From the fields came the rasping sound made by the mower as he whetted his scythe, before which the rich feathered grass and the wild flowers are done to death; elsewhere the joyous haymakers were hard at work, and the dust of June began to roll along the roads before the wind in the sunshine.

'June!' thought Eveline. 'Where will the winter find me?'

The preparations for her marriage were hurried on with a rapidity that appalled her; but, dear as the scheme was to Lady Aberfeldie, a somewhat unexpected event delayed that of Allan and Olive Raymond, and gave the Aberfeldie family once more something else to think of.

One evening when all the others were in Edinburgh save himself and Olive—for Eveline's forthcoming marriage kept all rather busy now—Allan, full of his own happy thoughts, and the joy that would be his ere long, was smoking in the grounds, when he was startled by a shrill cry that proceeded from an open window of the house—a French window that opened to the ground—and swift as light a man dashed past him and disappeared among the thick shrubberies.

'A thief!' was Allan's first thought; 'but whose cry was that?' was his second.

The face of the intruder, who passed near him—a pale and familiar one, seen just as Cameron had before seen it—seemed to be that of Hawke Holcroft.

'Impossible,' thought Allan, as he hurried towards the house; but it was not until he had further proofs that he became aware that the face he had seen—the face of ill-omen—was that of Holcroft!

He hurried into the apartment through the open window, and was horrified to find Olive prostrate on the floor, with her arms outspread, and in a fainting condition. He raised her up and laid her on a sofa, withdrawing the pillow from under her head, and looked round for water to lave her face and hands, one of which clutched a pen.

A large sealskin cigar case, with Rio Hondo cigars in it—a case which he well remembered to have seen in possession of Holcroft—lay upon the floor.

How came it there, unless the man he saw was, beyond all doubt, Hawke Holcroft?

Olive's cheque-book—for she had a bank account of her own—lay open on her davenport, and Allan's eye caught the counterfoil of one, dated that very day, and almost wet still, for £400.

'Four hundred pounds!' he gasped, and tried to tear open his necktie, while the room swam round him. 'Oh, God! can it be that she is playing fast and loose with me and that double-dyed villain?'

That she should have any intercourse, verbal or written, with such a wretch excited in Allan a gust of rage and bewilderment, disgust, horror, and intense perplexity.

Yet it might be all quite explainable—even the cheque.

She opened her eyes and closed them again, and pathetically he besought her to tell him what had happened, but could elicit no reply. Her slender throat seemed parched, as she failed to articulate.

'Oh, Olive,' said he, 'if I alarm you, forgive me. You know how I love you. Why torture me by this silence—tell me all—*what* has happened—*who* has been here?'

But he urged and pled in vain; her teeth were clenched.

'Is it some folly—some girlish imprudence? *what* is it? Dear love, only tell me?'

Still she was silent, and Allan's brows knit darkly and ominously, while, in the excited state of his nerves, he felt sharp twinges in the arm that had been fractured, and, when consciousness came partially back to Olive, she covered her face with her hands, and sobbed heavily and spasmodically.

What had happened? Why was she so suddenly cast down, hurled, as it were, from the joy, rapture, and repose of an hour ago, to the apparent agony and shame of the present?

Nothing could be elicited from her, and the next day found her in a species of hysterical fever, and in the hands of the doctor.

In a short time it was discovered that her cheque—an open one—payable to Mr. Hawke Holcroft, and duly endorsed by that personage, had been presented and cashed at a bank; yet no explanation could be elicited from her about it.

'She had on the ill-omened diamonds, mother,' said Allan, interrogatively. 'How was this?'

'I lent them to her, as the bride of the house, and doubtless she had been trying them on when—when——'

'This scoundrel thrust himself upon her presence?'

'I suppose so,' said Lady Aberfeldie, weeping.

'Evil always comes of these accursed stones!'

'It is simply outrageous,' said Lord Aberfeldie, sternly and loftily, 'that even the family of the most humble tradesman should be haunted by a Frankenstein—a swindler, and worse, like this—but that a house like mine—the house of a peer of the realm——'

And his lordship in his indignation paused as utterance failed him.

'Mystery is involved here,' exclaimed Lady Aberfeldie, 'and I dislike it intensely, as vulgar and very bad style.'

'By Jove, I should think so,' added Allan, gloomily; 'but this affair, like Cameron's marriage, beats the mysteries of Udolpho!'

CHAPTER XI.

'GUP,' AND WHAT CAME OF IT,

And now, ere it is too late, to let a little light on what must seem a mystery, and to tell a story which Eveline was not to hear until the fatal die was cast.

'Dear Evan,' said a handsome girl, as she interlaced her slender fingers on Cameron's arm lovingly in one of the most secluded walks of the Princes-Street Gardens, and under the shadow of the towering castle rock, 'I cannot bear to see you looking so unhappy—what *is* the matter?'

'Eveline Graham has ceased to meet me. She is ill—or—or I know not what!'

'Cannot you ascertain?'

'No. I have no means of ascertaining; moreover, only the other day she cut me.'

'Cut you—passed you?'

'Cut me dead!'

'Surely that was bad in taste.'

'And cruel too—so unlike her, Alice darling, that I know not what to think.'

'She has resolved to accept her rich old baronet—that is all; and I shall hear all about it when I am far away from you in India. How strange,' added the girl, dreamily, while a great, yet pensive, joy lighted up her blue eyes, 'how strange to think that I am still in Edinburgh, and so far away from *him*, when there was a time when I wondered if anyone in this world was ever so happy as I, when dear stupid Duncan asked me to be his wife! And oh, Evan dear, but for you and your great kindness to us, my heart must have broken and I should never have seen Duncan more!'

The fair speaker was the Alice whose name had unconsciously escaped Evan, as his heart was full of a great love and pity for her—the wife of his younger brother Duncan, from whom she had been separated in consequence of a foolish jealous quarrel, and having been, through that, sent home by him from India, had no other friend in Europe to whom to turn for succour and support than the kind-hearted, but half-penniless Laird of Stratherroch, who had at last effected an explanation and reconciliation between them.

When quartered in cantonments, in the first year of their marriage, not far from Hurdwar on the Ganges (where Allan got the idol he gave to Olive) there seemed to be no more loving and attached couple than Duncan Cameron and his little wife Alice, and both were prime favourites with the garrison; he, for his fine bearing which made him the pattern officer of his regiment—a Bengal Infantry corps—his skill in horsemanship, as a marksman and pigsticker, and his general *bonhomie* and good nature. She, for her beauty and sweetness, her great abundance of animal spirits, and a charming *espièglerie* that made her the object of attention from all.

Ladies were scarce in these cantonments so far 'up country,' and thus Alice proved a wonderful attraction to all the young subs at the band-stand, or on the racecourse, and elsewhere; and they hovered about her rather more than Duncan Cameron quite relished.

She was a leading feature at all the entertainments given by Sir Bevis Batardeau, G.C.S.I., the brigadier, and his wife; and indeed no ball, picnic, or dance was deemed complete without the presence of Alice Cameron.

Now, Sir Bevis was a notorious old *roué*, and the cause of much 'gup,' as scandal or gossip is called in India. He was a middle-aged man of fashion, grizzled and rather bald, with a reddish nose and wicked eyes, while Lady Batardeau, his senior by a year or two, was a kind and motherly woman, who loved Alice dearly; and 'gup' of course asserted that the General did so too, in a fashion of his own, and many things were said that never reached as yet the ears of Duncan Cameron.

The latter was sent to some distance from the cantonments on a particular duty, and poor Alice was left to mope in her bungalow alone.

'I often thought,' she said, 'if anything should ever separate us, I would die. The fear smote me like a sword's point, Evan, and the night Duncan left me a jackal howled fearfully in the compound. Was it ominous of evil? I fear so—for separated terribly we were fated to be, through no fault of mine.'

These forebodings made her pass sleeplessly the hot and breathless Indian nights while hourly the cantonment *ghurries* were clanged, and the jackals howled in the prickly hedges, and the mosquitoes seemed a thousand times more annoying—no chowrie would whisk them out of the muslin curtains; and her breakfast seemed so insipid now, and Gunga Ram, the *khansa-man*, or native butler, could find nothing to tempt her appetite; yet Gunga, though, like most Hindostanees, doubtful of the virtue of every European woman, was devoted to his own particular *mehm Sahib.*

Every morning she had been wont to watch at the open Venetian blinds of their bungalow for the handsome figure of Duncan returning from the early parade, while the sun was yet on the verge of the horizon; and every evening was spent together in delicious idleness—riding on the course, promenading by the band-stand, or wandering among the groves where the baubool breathes an exquisite perfume from its bells of gold, as the oleander does from its clusters of pink and white blossoms, and where the lovely little tailor-bird sews two leaves together and swings in his sweet-scented nest from the bough of some little tree.

Hourly she longed for the return of Duncan.

She was a petted favourite with Lady Batardeau, who, when calling on her one day, found her asleep under the verandah outside Cameron's bungalow on a long low Indian arm-chair.

Thinking how charming the girl-wife looked, Lady Batardeau, in playful kindness, slipped on one of her fingers a rose-diamond ring, which had been in the past time a gift to herself from Sir Bevis, when she valued his gifts more than she had reason to do now; and, having done this, she went softly and laughingly away.

To the joy of Alice, Cameron returned suddenly while she was yet puzzling herself to account for the presence of the ring, and for a time, in the happiness of their reunion, she forgot all about it, till he, while toying with her pretty hands, observed it on her finder.

'A magnificent ring, Alice,' said he. 'Where did it come from?'

'That is more than I can tell you.'

'How?' he asked.

'I found that it had been slipped on my finger when I was asleep.'

'By whom?'

'I cannot say, Duncan dear.'

On examining the jewel he saw graven on the inside the name of that notorious old *roué* and Lothario, the brigadier!

Lady Batardeau had left the cantonments for awhile, and poor Alice could give no explanation as to how the mysterious ring with the name of Sir Bevis thereon came to be on her finger. Duncan loved her so trustfully, so utterly, that doubt failed for a time to find a place in his gallant heart; but 'gup' had playfully asserted that the old brigadier immensely admired young Mrs. Cameron—he recalled some jests he had heard, and now the poison they breathed was stealing upon his senses, and his face grew white as death.

Duncan mistook the genuine confusion of Alice for guilt—her dismay for dread of detection, and the whole affair for a feature in an intrigue. He knew how keen and bitter was scandal in India, and already he saw himself a source of mockery and disgrace, and figuring, perhaps, in the columns of the *Hurkara*!

He saw it all now! He had been sent on duty to a distance for some days, as he believed out of his turn, and by the express order of the brigadier.

That circumstance had surprised him, but he believed it was fully explained now by finding the ring of Sir Bevis on his wife's finger, and he became transported with fury. Alice cowered for a time beneath the expression she read in his face.

Could it be possible, he thought, that she was proving as one of the 'dead-sea apples of life, which a mocking fate so often throws in our lap, charming to the imagination, but bitter to the sense?'

'Duncan!' said Alice, softly and imploringly; but he felt all the mute despair of a broken heart, the agony of a shaken faith, and he put her soft white hands gently from him, as if he would never seek them in this life again.

He at once sought the presence of the brigadier, who, on hearing what he had to say, certainly—to do him justice—was rather bewildered.

'I beg leave, sir, to return to you this ring,' said Duncan, tossing it contemptuously on the table.

'My ring—my wife's ring it was—'

'*Was*—eh!'

'Yes, Captain Cameron. Where did you find it?'

'Where you placed it, I doubt not.'

'I do not understand your tone and manner, Captain Cameron; but I certainly placed it on the finger——'

'Of my wife,' said Duncan, hoarsely and scornfully. 'I thank you for your kind attention, but trust that it will end here ere worse come of it. I am not a man to be trifled with, Sir Bevis.'

Now, Sir Bevis had no dislike to be thought 'a gay Lothario, a sad dog, and all that sort of thing,' so he actually simpered provokingly, shrugged his shoulders and said, deprecatingly,

'Really, you wrong Mrs. Cameron.'

'She has deceived me!' exclaimed Duncan, furiously.

'If a woman can't deceive her own husband, *whom* may she deceive!' asked the unwise brigadier.

'In the days of the pistol this matter would not have ended here.'

'Come, come, don't let you and I fall to carte and tierce in this fashion,' said the general; 'it may be explainable——'

'I want no explanations!'

'As you please. It seems there is a little romance in most lives——'

'With your grey hairs you should have outlived all that, I think.'

Now his years proved a sore point with old Sir Bevis, and he became inflamed with anger; but, ere he could retort, Duncan had jerked his sword under his left arm and swept from his presence with a rather withering expression in his face, and that very evening saw Alice in the train for Delhi, *en route* to Europe.

'Innocent, I suffer all the shame and all the agony of guilt! Oh, it is hard, Duncan—very, very hard,' were the last words she said, brokenly, to her husband, who heard her with a stern silence that astonished her.

Now that Lady Batardeau, on her return to the cantonments, had explained the whole story of the ring, Duncan was—when too late, for his wife was on the sea—full of shame and contrition for his suspicions and severity, and had written to crave the pardon of Alice and insure her return to him again; hence the farewell and departure of 'Mrs. Cameron,' with her overlands and other baggage, as witnessed by the sharp little eyes of Sir Paget Puddicombe at the Waverley Station, and thus it was that, by an unexplained mistake, two fond hearts were separated for ever; but separated they would have been eventually by fate or fortune—the lack of fortune, rather—as time may show.

But for a time poor Eveline had to ponder bitterly on the humiliating thought that Evan Cameron had been thinking of *another* face, form, and name while in the act of caressing herself, and that the other was—as Sir Paget had left them no reason to doubt, and never himself doubted—Evan Cameron's wife!

CHAPTER XII.

OLIVE'S VISITOR,

Another mystery has now to be accounted for—the state in which Allan found Olive when her cry reached him as he idled with his cigar in the grounds at Maviswood in the evening, when the rest of the family circle were in town.

Olive was seated alone in one of the drawing-rooms when a gentleman was announced—a gentleman who no doubt thought Allan was absent in Edinburgh also.

'Mr. Holcroft.'

'Mr. Holcroft!' A book she was reading fell from the hand of Olive, and she started to her feet as that personage, hat in hand, stood smilingly before her. For a moment she could scarcely believe her eyes as they met the pale, watery, and shifty ones of her unexpected visitor.

Terror and horror filled her heart on finding herself face to face with this man—an assassin in intent! It was too horrible—too *outré* and grotesque to think of.

But what was his intention now? She was not left long in ignorance. Why did she not rush to the bell—summon the household, and have the daring intruder expelled or arrested? But no—she felt a very coward just then, with a great dread of Allan discovering him, and a heavy, sickening foreboding of coming evil.

There came dreamily to her memory, too, some threatening words of his when he had said that he would let no man come between them, and that, though he might fail to compel her to love him, he might compel her to marry him: but neither love nor marriage were in the mind of her horrible visitor just then.

Mr. Hawke Holcroft seemed rather 'down on his luck,' and looked somewhat shabby and seedy. The last fragment of his patrimony had been swallowed up; his betting-book had proved a mistake, as he had for some time past backed the wrong horses; cards had failed him and play of all kinds; in short, he was desperate, and hence his appearance at Maviswood.

To attempt the role of a lover again, after all that had passed, and after all that he was aware must be known to Miss Raymond, was, he knew, impossible; but he had a trump card to play in the way of extortion—plain, blunt, rascally extortion; so, conceiving that the girl was utterly alone, he could not for the life of him resist bantering her a little, all the more as the utter loathing and dread her face expressed, enraged him.

'Mr. Holcroft!' she exclaimed, in a breathless voice, as she recoiled and became white as a lily.

'Yes, Hawke Holcroft, the man your fatal beauty has made him,' said he, with melodramatic gloom and folded arms; 'when I met you first I met my fate—a love that was my doom. But for you, would I ever have been mad enough to attempt the life of Allan Graham?'

'How dare you come here—how dare you speak to me thus!' said Olive, glancing at the bell handle; but he planted himself between it and her.

'The love of you came to me when first you looked into my face,' he resumed, in his melodramatic style; 'I remember it was but a smile—a smile; yet a mist came before my eyes—a something stirred my heart. Ah, Olive Raymond, it was your beautiful eyes that suddenly kindled new life within me—that will only end with the old.'

Olive was more irritated than alarmed now.

'How dare you come here?' she asked.

'I can't help it—needs must when old Boots drives,' said he; 'I came to show you a work of art. Look here.'

From his pocket-book he drew out and held before her at arm's length the cabinet photo of herself in a ball-dress; the photo, or one like it, that she had the folly to give him at Dundargue; but to her horror and dismay she saw that it had been reproduced, reversed, and manipulated in some way by some low photographer, and combined with one of Holcroft himself, posed as if in the act of embracing her, forming a strange group of two, whose likenesses there would be no mistaking, more especially that of her, as it was a miraculous work of art in its truth and individuality.

It was Olive to the life, with her brightest and sweetest expression now bent on his face!

'I am glad you recognise us,' said he, mockingly, as he replaced the photo in its receptacle, and the latter in his breast pocket; 'and now to business. What would your drawing-room hero think of this, if he saw it? Ha, ha! He did not approve of Byron at Dundargue, I remember—would rather we stuck to Dr. Watts' hymns, I suppose—'How doth the little busy bee," and so forth; well, like that industrious insect, I mean to improve "the shining hour." How would he—how will you and your family, with all their cursed Scotch pride—like to see this photo in every shop window exposed for sale to the British public, among ballet-girls in snowstorms, countesses swinging in hammocks, bishops, and generals—murderers, too, perhaps—eh? In a week or two I may have a million copies of this precious photo for sale in London and elsewhere. Do you realise the meaning of this, my scornful beauty? and the result it must have on you, your name, your character, your family, and your future—Miss Olive Raymond posed in the arms of Hawke Holcroft?'

'Oh, heavens!' said Olive, in a low voice like a whisper; 'are you a man or a devil?'

'A little of both, perhaps—I am what circumstances have made me.'

'Daring wretch—oh, what wrong have I ever done you that you should cross my path and agonise me thus?'

Holcroft laughed; he knew that she had a more than handsome allowance at her guardian's behest and her own bank account. He was without remorse or pity, for cowardice and selfishness were alike the ruling features of his character, and he thought to control the tongue and action of Olive through her own pride and her love of Allan with an eye to future monetary extortions.

Pressing her left hand upon her heart, as if she felt—as no doubt she did—a spasm of pain there, and, with her eyes almost closed, she said,

'In the name of mercy, give me back that photo!'

'After I have had it so carefully improved as a work of art? No; no, Miss Raymond,' said he, in his detestable sneering tone; 'but I shall be content to forego my interest in the copyright for a certain reasonable consideration.'

'A consideration. I do not understand you, sir,' said Olive, faintly, and clutching a table for support.

'Plainly, then, I mean a cheque for three hundred—no, let me say four hundred—pounds, and you had better be quick about it, as I have no time to spare, and, truth to tell, have no desire to renew my acquaintance with any of the Aberfeldie folks again.'

'Four hundred pounds?'

'That is the sum, Miss Raymond.'

Like a blind person, she feebly and irresolutely seemed to grope with her key about the lock of her davenport, and Holcroft said,

'Permit me to assist you.'

He unlocked it, and threw open the lid. Mechanically she seated herself, and began to write, while conscious that this bantering villain was still addressing her.

'And so old Puddicombe has come to the front again,' said he. 'An odd marriage it will be—his with Miss Graham—Brummagem allying itself with the Middle Ages—the counting-house getting a line in Burke's Peerage.'

'There,' said she, handing him the cheque, which he received with a low mocking bow, 'now give me the photo.'

'Thanks, with pleasure. Perhaps you may wish to frame it. Now, listen to me,' he said, through his set teeth, 'if you divulge a word of this interview, or make known the power I have over you by means of this photograph, "then and in that case," as I believe your father's will is phrased, I shall at once introduce it to the British public. I give you this copy for your four hundred pounds, but retain the negative!'

Then it was that, as he withdrew, a cry escaped from her overcharged breast—the cry overheard by Allan, and she had only power left her to conceal the odious photo in the breast of her dress, when she fell fainting on the floor, where she was found.

To destroy it was one of her first acts, when consciousness returned, and she was alone; but what availed the destruction of this one, when her tormentor possessed the power of producing others without limit?

A great horror possessed her now—a dread and gloom came over her, with a painful nervous terror—a kind of hunted emotion—a fear of what might next ensue!

Yet she took no one into her confidence, not even Allan—on her part a fatal error.

After all her past sweet intercourse with him, their delayed marriage—delayed by the illness incident to Holcroft's outrage—and his too probable speedy departure on foreign service, was she now to harrow him up by a reference to her folly, her petulance, and her silly degrading flirtation with this man, who now proved such a pitiful, such an unfathomable villain!

What if Allan should see suddenly that fatal photo in a shop window? This possibility plainly stared her in the face; yet she was silent, and believed that ere this issue came to pass, she was doomed to be tortured and victimised by Holcroft again; and the thought, the fear of this, gave her a kind of fever of the spirit, which made her quite ill, and bewildered her friends.

Money had evidently been given by her to Holcroft—no small sum too; and for what purpose? Remembering his threat if she exposed his rascality, her tongue was now tied by a most unwise terror. Ill and harrassed, she remained much in her room and avoided society.

Allan, as he said resentfully, failed 'to see the situation,' and in a gust of pique and anger, feeling himself somewhat degraded by Olive's bearing, resigned his extended leave and joined his regiment, as Olive said, resolved to 'sulk in Edinburgh Castle, rather than have an explanation,' rather unreasonably forgetting that she had steadily refused to give one.

She felt painfully that the mystery of the money given to Holcroft was calculated to compromise her with her kindred; but what was that when compared with the awful thundercloud which hung over her, if he made the public use he threatened of the photo!

Her soul died within her. Meanwhile Allan struggled hard to make himself believe that he might yet be happy with Olive; that he had perhaps no solid reason for being otherwise; but it would not do.

'Hang it, what does all this new mystery mean?' he would say to himself. 'We seem fated to misunderstand each other somehow. After all, she seems to love her pride more than me, still!'

And Olive knew that it was mingled pride and fear that had opened a kind of chasm between her and Allan again; yet a little sense, a little courage and candour, might have closed it speedily enough, and smoothed away the anger the complication raised at times within her; while to Allan the situation was certainly an intolerable one, and Olive's silence or reticence made it all the more so.

CHAPTER XIII.

WEDDED.

While baffled in her attempts to bring about an explanation between Allan and Olive, and to smooth matters over with that wilful young lady (as she deemed her) and her naturally irritated *fiancé*, Lady Aberfeldie pushed on vigorously all the arrangements for the marriage of Sir Paget and the ill-starred Eveline—a marriage for which there seemed then no other reason than an avaricious desire of grand settlements and so forth.

All Olive's old pride and petulance (with much of irritation that was new) seemed to have come back to her, and, until the matter was cleared up regarding that mysterious visit of Holcroft to Maviswood, Allan had ceased to speak of marriage, and thus her spirit took fire at being doubted and humbled.

She shrank, unwisely, from a simple confession that might have obviated all this, and from revealing the shame and affront to which this man possessed the power of exposing her.

'I detest riddles, and care not to read them; but the mask she is wearing—if a mask it be—may prove a costly one for herself and us all,' thought Lord Aberfeldie and his son too.

'Be content, Allan, to know that I gave that money—a trifle to me—to Mr. Holcroft in the hope to save us all—especially myself—from a probable public affront which might destroy me,' said Olive on one occasion, her eyes flashing through her tears.

'What mystery is this?—what can you have done? how be in his power? The assertion is absurd!'

'Allan, cannot you trust me?' she asked, fondly and sadly, yet proudly.

'I know not what to think, but the whole affair looks—looks to me——'

'How.'

'Well, devilish queer,' said he, as he cut the matter short, and rode away, on which Olive dried her tears, crested up her head, and looked defiant.

'If this tiresome couple, Olive and Allan, continue to pout and sulk at each other,' said Lady Aberfeldie; 'and he should decline to marry her, her money may be lost to us by her twenty-fifth birthday.'

'Unless——' the lord twisted his moustache and paused.

'Unless what?'

'Allan gets himself killed in Egypt,' replied Lord Aberfeldie, grimly.

'Good heavens, do not say such a thing, even in jest!'

And now, perforce of their present situation, a change had come over the two cousins, Olive and Eveline—they never read, studied, sung, rode, or walked together, as they had been wont to do; a blight had come over both their lives apparently.

Eveline only felt a little at ease when Sir Paget was absent from her, and even then she was pestered by his love-letters, which, like those written usually by men of advanced years, were of a grotesquely impassioned nature. 'Attachments at that age are deeper, and less anxiety not to compromise oneself is shown and felt,' says an essayist. 'After fifty, men are often wise enough to vote the writing of love-letters a bore, but some carry on the practice to a very advanced age. Their protestations are then ingeniously flavoured with touches of the paternal, which sometimes entirely mislead the unsophisticated recipients.'

But the mere sight of Sir Paget's caligraphy, and of his heraldic note-paper, having a shield with some mysterious design thereon, and the motto *Puddicombe petit alta!* (Puddicombe seeks lofty objects), proved always enough for Eveline, who tossed it into the waste-paper basket unread, but torn into minute fragments, while a sigh of weariness and repugnance escaped her.

Evan Cameron loved Allan Graham dearly as a friend, and had naturally a desire to be on the best terms with him as the brother of the girl to whom he had given all his heart. Thus, while meeting him daily on parade and at mess, he was sorely puzzled to account for the change he felt in Allan's manner to himself, as he knew not that the latter resented the 'Mrs. Cameron' episode as an insult to Eveline, his sister.

'I presume you know that my sister is on the point of marriage—indeed, that the day is fixed?' said Allan, rather grimly, to him one day as he recalled the circumstance of how Evan greatly admired, to say the least of it, Eveline, and how her heart had responded thereto.

Cameron made no reply, but a sudden pallor overspread his handsome, bronzed face, and all his studied calmness forsook him, while the memory of past hopes and joys shook his heart as if with a tempest of remembrance; but, stooping and half turning away to conceal the expression of his face, he attempted to light a cigar.

'What a sly fellow—a cunning dog—you are!' said Allan, with irritation of tone.

'In what way do you mean, Allan?' asked Cameron.

'Mean! How dare you ask, after your open admiration of my sister, Miss Graham, in a man in your position?'

Cameron mistook his meaning; but the mistake failed to rouse any pride, as his heart was too crushed and sore just then.

'Allan!' he exclaimed, as tears almost welled up in his honest eyes, 'I loved her—I love her still—God alone knows how well, how desperately, and how hopelessly.'

'Hopelessly indeed,' responded Allan, his cheek now aflame with anger; 'and you dare to tell me this after all that we know of yourself and Mrs. Cameron?'

It was now Cameron's turn to look indignant and astonished; but in a few words he explained all.

'Poor Evan!' said Allan, as he wrung the hand of Cameron, whose head sank forward, so much was he overcome by emotion; 'I am glad of this explanation, but it comes too late—if indeed it could ever have served any purpose so far as your hopes with Eveline are concerned. In three days she is to be married—and now, let us talk of the subject no more.'

But for a time black fury gathered in the heart of Cameron at Sir Paget Puddicombe, whose deductions, however, from all that he saw at the railway station, were most natural.

'In three days,' he muttered again and again, 'in three days, and she will be lost to me for ever!'

Eveline as yet was ignorant of her lover's purity and innocence, nor would the knowledge of it have availed her much. There was a meek abandonment of her own will—of her own judgment, and Lady Aberfeldie caressed her more than she had ever done before, glad to find that she had become—my lady cared not why or how—compliant at last.

She seemed quite passive and supine—resigned, Olive phrased it—and ready to do her mother's bidding, for Evan Cameron seemed to have quite passed out of her life, though the name 'Alice' he had uttered seemed to be ever in her ears.

She heard her mother speaking, and felt her caresses, but her eyes were suffused by a kind of mist. Yet more than once she had started amid her apathy, and thought, 'Why am I still here—why don't I run away to where they will never find me?'

But she had no determining motive to decide her choice of place or scheme of life, though she felt that ere long, when these last three days were past, she would have to reconstruct her entire future, and from that future her heart recoiled and shrank. Her temples throbbed as she thought of this; her heart seemed alternately to thunder in her breast, and then to become unnaturally still.

Again and again her mother told her that she would be surrounded by such wealth as falls to the lot of few; but she cared not for wealth, nor would it ever remove her gloomy and bitter reflections, and at the very name of her intended husband, though she evinced no emotion, a secret and involuntary shudder came over her.

Society was intolerable just then, and she had much of it at Maviswood. How intolerable seemed lawn-tennis amid the bright sunshine, the soft thud of the balls upon the racquets, as they were shot over the nettings from court to court, the laughter of young and sweet voices, and the cries ever and anon of 'fifteen,' 'thirty,' 'fault,' and so on, as the jovial game progressed; and with evening came the inevitable dinner-party, and at night the dance.

Allan, fearing to lacerate his sister's heart, knew not how to undeceive her in the matter of Cameron's supposed duplicity, though the truth or falsehood thereof could not affect her fate or her relations with Sir Paget now; but the true story escaped Carslogie quite casually when in conversation with Olive, who in due time related it to Eveline, in whose breast it created some very mingled emotions.

So Evan was innocent, while she had been feeling in her heart all the passion and pain—yea, a sentiment of vengeance—which women will feel, when they believe they have been loving unworthily.

Early on her marriage morning she left her bed to think over all this. Wrapped in a snow-white *peignoir* (or dressing-robe), with all her undressed hair floating about her shoulders and blown back by the warm summer breeze, she sat at the open window of her room, and looked dreamily out with sad, sad eyes on the sunny landscape and the lovely hills all steeped in golden haze.

How changed seemed its beauty now, and how she longed to be away from it—to be dead, in fact! Yet she was at an age when even to live, ought to be in itself a joy.

The fragrance of the dewy summer morning seemed to fill the outer world, and amid the intense stillness she heard only the voices of a lark high in the air and of a cushat dove in the coppice.

Her marriage morning—what a morning of woe to her! Her cheeks were pale—very, very pale; but with her parted scarlet lips, and her tangled waves of rich brown hair, she was beautiful as ever.

The knowledge that her lover had not deceived her, but was true, roused her for a time, and filled her soul with a tempest of unexpected sorrow, compunction, and joy—sorrow that she had wronged him, compunction for the cruel mode in which she had treated him, and joy that his honour was unstained, and that he still was true; but oh! what must he think of her?

Burying her face in her tremulous white hands, she wept like a child—-wept as we are told 'only women weep when their hearts break over the grave of a dead love,' and threw herself across her bed.

'God forgive me—God forgive me, and bless and comfort you, my love,' she murmured. 'Oh, Evan, I have wronged you—wronged you; but what does it avail us after all—after all?'

And she lay there crouched and gathered in a heap, as it were, till Olive and others who were to be her bridesmaids roused her and lifted her up and summoned Clairette.

So her marriage-day had come, and, unless she fell ill or died, the ceremony was to go inexorably on.

Olive was far from well; every day she expected to hear of Holcroft's photo being seen; her sole protection against that catastrophe as yet, was the fear that ere it came to pass, he would seek her presence at least once again, on an errand of extortion. But ill or well, she had to bear her part in the ceremony as a bridesmaid, and a charming one she looked.

Allan, of course, was there too, but not as groomsman—a 'fogie' friend of Sir Paget officiated in that capacity, and more than once did the head of the latter jerk about in a way that was quite alarming as he entered the church, which was *en fête* for the occasion.

To the tortured mind of his bride, she thought it would be a relief when the ceremony was over, and the phantasmagoria that seemed to surround her had all passed away. 'Is not certainty better than suspense?' asks Rhoda Broughton; 'night better than twilight? despair than the sickly flicker of an extinguishing hope?'

'In marrying in this compulsory fashion, I do this poor man a great wrong,' thought Eveline, 'and condemn myself to a life-long sorrow.'

And amid the sacrifice Lady Aberfeldie, calm and aristocratic, stood with a great air of dignity and grace peculiarly her own.

'She will love Sir Paget in time, if love is necessary,' she was thinking; 'he is so good, so generous, and *so* rich.'

So rich—yes, with her—there lay the magnet and the secret of it all!

The bridesmaids, all handsome girls, were uniformly costumed; among them amber-haired Ruby Logan, quite jubilant with reviving hopes of Allan.

Eveline's cold and now white lips murmured almost inaudibly the words she was bidden to say—the few but terrible words that made her a wedded wife—while her pallid face was but half seen amid the bridal veil, that seemed to float like filmy mist around her. Allan alone, who knew the real secret of her heart, looked pityingly, darkly, and gravely on, for it was a union of which—however his father and mother desired it—he did not approve.

For a time Eveline had actually schooled herself to think that marriage would give her a species of vengeance on the man who, she thought, had wronged and oppressed her. But now, oh, heaven! she loved the lost one more than ever, while death alone could unforge the fetters her lips were riveting.

Was it ominous of evil that the ring dropped from her wedding finger as Sir Paget placed it there?

At last all was over. The great organ pealed forth the wedding-march. The bells rang joyously in the great spire overhead, and she was led forth by Sir Paget, leaning on his arm, a wedded wife.

So time would pass on—days dawn and nights close; the moon would shine amid the fleecy clouds on the quiet pastoral hills, on the great castellated mass of Dundargue, the woods and waters of her old home; but never would she be as she had been—as a happy, thoughtless girl—the Eveline Graham of the past years; never more could joy be hers, or would she know again the love she had lost, the tenderness she had tasted; and times there were when, amid her general passive appearance of numbness and indifference, hot, scorching tears of utter despair escaped her, and a passionate longing seized her to take to flight, whither she knew not, and to rend asunder the meshes of the marriage net that bound her now; and in this frame of mind she departed on her honeymoon!

On that morning, there lingered long on one of the western batteries of the old castle an officer who—if he was noticed at all—seemed to be solely intent on enjoying a cigar, and who seemed to avoid the society of all.

This was poor Evan Cameron, listening to the wedding bells in the distant spire, and well he knew for what a tragedy they were ringing; and, each time their clangour came upon the wind, they seemed to find an echo in his heart.

So she was married at last, and more than ever lost to him!

Cards came to him in due course, and he tore them into minute fragments.

Evan did all his regimental duties and daily work like a man—but as one in a dream—all that was required of him, with more than ever, if possible, strict punctilio; yet he felt himself a mere machine, without heart or soul; and had only one longing, for the time when he might turn his back upon his native country, and find himself face to face with the enemy, no matter who, or where, that enemy might be.

CHAPTER XIV.

MISTRUST.

'Now that dear Eveline is off our hands,' said Lady Aberfeldie, 'I cannot help thinking seriously of Allan's affairs and those of Olive, and really some serious advice should be given to the foolish couple. Could not you——'

'No,' interrupted her husband; 'I wash my hands of lovers and their piques and plans. You have managed the matter of Eveline and Sir Paget—try your skill once more.'

'Neither Allan nor Olive is so compliant as poor Eveline.'

'No—poor Eveline indeed!'

'You think of her marriage thus, now?'

'Well, there is no denying it is rather a January-and-May style of thing; but let us not speak of it.'

Considering that her husband had from the first given his full assent to the whole transaction, Lady Aberfeldie could not help glancing at him rather reproachfully, but she only said,

'Olive has, of course, many admirers; but the rumour of her engagement to Allan keeps them all at a distance.'

'Poor Olive! Her fortune is almost a misfortune to her.'

'Why?'

'She imagines it to be the attraction of everyone, rather than her own beauty.'

'And once she conceived it to be the attraction of Allan; but she knows better now—that he loves, or loved, her for herself alone.'

'She has already had two peers and a baronet in her train, all drawn thither, I fear, by her money-bags alone, and young Carslogie of Ours seemed desperately smitten, too.'

'Ours?'

'Well, I always think of the Black Watch as 'Ours'—it is force of habit—a good-looking fellow, well-born, well-bred, with plenty of money.'

'Allan is his equal in all these and more; but what he and she mean by dallying and delaying as they do, I cannot conceive.'

Allan had looked upon Olive at the recent marriage in her striking costume as a bridesmaid, and thought she had never appeared to greater advantage.

Why should she not have figured there as a bride too? What was the secret spring of this doubt and mistrust that had come between them again, and which she shrank from attempting to explain?

To do her justice, she was often on the point of doing so; but a sentiment of miserable fear of what Allan might do, think, or say, if made aware of the deep affront Holcroft was capable of inflicting upon his future wife, tied her tongue.

Better would it have been a thousand times had she trusted to Allan fully and implicitly, and to the means he might put in force to procure or purchase the silence for ever of such a reptile as her tormentor.

The knowledge in the minds of both, that a time for separation must inevitably come soon now, if all the rumours of war proved true, softened their emotions, and drew the cousins towards each other again.

The intercourse between them had, as of old, its usual charm, but was strange and constrained, for as Allan did not attempt again the *rôle* of lover, but seemed to 'bide his time,' Olive felt her pride alarmed, and would often reply to him coldly, with a straightening of her slim form, and a cresting up of her graceful neck and handsome head.

Time passed on; she heard nothing of Hawke Holcroft or his threats, and the courage of Olive rose; but it was awful to think of her name being at the mercy of such a creature, even if she were married!

Once the love that was really smouldering in the hearts of both nearly burst into a flame again.

Olive was seated in the garden at Maviswood so deeply lost in thought that she was unaware of Allan's approach until he overhung the rustic sofa she occupied.

'A penny for your thoughts, Olive,' said he.

'The sum usually offered for what might prove a perilous secret to know.'

'Well?'

'My thoughts were of many things till your voice scattered them,' said she, twirling her sunshade on her shoulder.

'I was in hope they were of—me.'

Olive only smiled, and remained silent, while he looked into her eyes with a curiously mingled expression, which seemed to be both imploring and commanding, but she only said,

'They were not of you—why should they be?'

Allan drew back a pace, with a cloudy brow.

'Forgive my being playful for a moment, Olive—I shall never in this way offend you again.'

She gave him a sweet and deprecating, almost an entreating, glance; but Allan did not perceive it; his face was turned angrily and sadly from her, so her pique—ever so ready—became roused.

'Olive,' said Allan, after a pause, 'love should always be stronger than pride.'

'Of course—when love exists,' she replied, turning a shoulder from him.

'And with you, Olive, do not let it stand between us as before. If your father's will is again the cause, let me tell you once more that I refuse to have any share in that lunatic arrangement, and will not marry you on any such conditions.'

'Who is thinking or talking of marriage?' said she, sarcastically, yet making an effort to restrain her tears; 'moreover, I fear that as a husband you would be very tyrannical and cruel.'

'My character in the present and the past does not bear out this, I think.'

'Suspicious, then?'

'Not without extreme and just reason,' replied Allan, as his mind flashed back to the Holcroft episode.

She strove to glance at him defiantly, but failing, smiled, though his handsome face had in it an expression of sorrow and anger.

'Ere a month be past, Olive, an Egyptian bullet may make you every way a free woman, so far as regards your father's will.'

'I do not wish to be free from it,' she was on the point of saying passionately, but controlled her speech and remained—unwisely—silent.

Allan regarded her wistfully.

'Are injudicious reticence and a little aversion the best beginning of a true love?' he asked.

'Perhaps—I am no casuist,' said she, tapping the ground with a pretty little foot impatiently.

Lovely, pouting, and wistful, her face was now turned to his with a mixture of petulance and shy reproach as she thought,

'Oh, why does he not take me in his arms, and kiss and make a fuss with me as he used to do.'

But, repelled by her curious manner, Allan had no intention of doing any such thing, and thought her a curious enigma. So thus the chance of a complete reunion ended, and ere long the luckless Olive was to have cause for repenting most bitterly her lack of candour and perfect trust, and the force of the overweening pride which engendered mistrust in one who loved her so well.

CHAPTER XV.

THE BLACK WATCH.

War with Egypt had been declared, and in the Castle of Edinburgh, as in every other fortress and barrack in the British Isles, the notes of preparation were sounding, and the Black Watch, ever so glorious in the annals of our army, was among the regiments bound for the land where, eighty years before, it had gathered such a crop of laurels under the gallant Abercrombie, in conflict, not against a feeble horde of Egyptians, but when encountering forty thousand of the veteran infantry of France.

From that day in the October of 1739 when the companies of *Freicudan Dhu*, or Black Watch (so called from their sombre green tartans), drawn from the Munroes of Ross, the Grants of Strathspey, and the Campbells of Lochnelland Carrick, were first enrolled as a regiment on the Birks of Aberfeldie, near the southern bank of the Tay, by the gallant old Earl of Crawford, the 42nd has been second to none in peace and war, and its very name and number are rendered dear to the people of Scotland by innumerable ties of friendship and clanship, by traditions and glorious exploits in battle.

In almost everything that has added strength or brilliance to the British Empire the regiment has borne a leading part, and to attempt to trace its annals would be to write the history of our wars since the days of the second George.

Suffice it that the second year after the companies were constituted a regiment, saw them fighting for the House of Austria against France and Bavaria, and covering the rear of that British army which was hurled from the heights of Fontenoy by the bayonets of the Irish Brigades, and where, we are told, 'the gallantry of Sir Robert Munroe of 'the gallantry of Sir Robert Munroe of Culcairn and his Highlanders was the theme of admiration through all Britain.'

So it was with them in the old Flanders war, till 1758 saw them attacking Ticonderoga in America, where, rushing from amid the Reserve, where they disdained to linger, they hewed down the dense abatis with their claymores, and, storming the breastworks, 'climbing up one another's shoulders, and placing their feet in the holes made in the face of the works by their swords and bayonets, no ladders having been provided,' exposed the while to a dreadful fire of cannon and musketry, under which six hundred and forty-seven of them fell; and hence a cry for vengeance went through the country of the clans, procuring so many recruits, and another battalion was formed, and fresh glories were won in the West India Isles, where, at Martinique and by the walls of the Moro, their pipes sent up the notes of victory.

In the fatal strife of the American revolt they were ever in the van, and the first years of the present century saw their tartans waving darkly amid the battle-smoke of Aboukir, under the shadow of Pompey's Pillar, and on the plains of Alexandria, where they cut to pieces the French Invincibles, slew six hundred and fifty of them, captured their colours, which were delivered to Major Stirling, together with the cannon they had also seized; and ere long the mosques and towers of Grand Cairo echoed to their martial music.

Who can record the brilliance of their valour in the long and glorious war of the Peninsula—that war of victories, which began on the banks of the Douro and continued to the hill of Toulouse? And anon, their never-to-be-forgotten prowess on the plains of Waterloo, when, under Macara, they formed the flower of Picton's superb division, and where, with the Greys and Gordon Highlanders, they sent up the cry which still finds echo in every Scottish heart, the *cri-de-guerre* of 'Scotland for ever!' while plunging into those mighty French columns, which rolled away before their bayonets like smoke before the wind.

There their total casualties were two hundred and ninety-seven of all ranks.

'They fought like heroes, and like heroes fell—an honour to the country,' to quote the War Office Record, page 145. 'On many a Highland hill, and through many a Lowland valley, long will the deeds of these brave men be fondly remembered and their fate deeply deplored. Never did a finer body of men take the field; never did men march to battle that were destined to perform such services to their country, and to obtain such immortal renown.'

But equal renown did their services win on the banks of the Alma, when old Colin Campbell led them into action, exclaiming,

'Now, men, the whole army is watching us; make me proud of my Highland Brigade!'

And reason indeed had that grand old soldier to be proud of his lads in the kilt, as they swept up the green hillsides to glory. 'The ground they had to ascend,' says an eye-witness, the author of 'Eothen,' 'was a good deal more steep and broken than the slope beneath the redoubt. In the land where those Scots were bred, there are shadows of sailing clouds shimmering up the mountain side, and their paths are rugged and steep, yet their course is smooth, easy, and swift. Smoothly, easily, and swiftly the Black Watch seemed to glide up the hill. A few minutes before their tartans ranged dark in the valley; now their plumes were on the crest.'

Into the dense grey masses of the Kazan column, over which towered the miraculous figure of St. Sergius, their steady volley swept like a sheet of lead; anon their line of bayonets was flashing to the charge like a hedge of steel, and a wail of despair broke from the Muscovites, who, crying that 'the Angel of Death had come,' threw away all that might impede their speed and fled.

'Then,' says the brilliant author we have quoted, 'rose the cheers of the Highland Brigade. Along the Kourgané slopes, and thence west almost home to the causeway, the hillsides were made to resound with that joyous and assuring cry, which is the natural utterance of a northern people so long as it is warlike and free.'

Their furious onset struck terror to many an Indian heart during the dark years of the Sepoy revolt, and like sweetest music their pipes were heard by that desperate and despairing band who fought for their wives and children in beleaguered Lucknow; and as, of course, the old Black Watch must be in everything, they bore their share in the conquest of Coomassie, and were the first men in the sable city, as their pipes announced to the army of Wolseley.

While on this subject, we cannot help quoting a Frenchman's estimate of the Scottish troops. In the *Moniteur de Soir* for 1868, a writer says,

'The Scottish soldiers form without distinction the cream of the British army, and the Highlander is the prototype of the excellent soldier. He has all the requisite qualities without one defect. Unluckily for Great Britain, the population of Scotland is not numerous. Saving, it is true, to the point of putting by penny after penny, the Scotsman, for all that, is honest, steadfast, and amiable in his intercourse with others, enthusiastic and proud, most chivalrous when the question is about shedding his blood. The old traditions of clanship subsist, each company is grouped round an illustrious name, and all and every man is sure to be the captain's cousin. The Highlanders have a strange sort of bravery, which partakes of French fire and English phlegm. They rush with impetuosity, they charge with vigour, but are not hurried away by anger. In the very hottest of an attack, a simple order suffices to stop them. Formed in square, you would take them for Englishmen, but in the bayonet charge you would swear they were French. For the rest they are of Celtic origin, and the blood of our fathers flows in their veins. In the eyes of the Turk, the Scots have one enormous fault—that of showing their bare legs. In *our* eyes they have but one defect, but still excessively annoying—their depraved taste for the screaming of the bagpipes. We know that the Highlanders would not get under fire (with *élan*) without being excited by their national airs being played on this discordant instrument. One of their generals having put down this piercing music, they attacked the enemy so languidly that the bagpipes had to be restored to them, and then they took the position. In a word, we repeat that the Scots are magnificent soldiers.'

We may smile at the Frenchman's idea of the pipes, for as the old piper said of Count Flauhault when he expressed his disgust thereat, 'Maybe she heard owre muckle o' them at Waterloo.'

And now once again the Black Watch were going to the land of the sun and the desert, where Abercrombie received his death-wound while calling to them in the charge, 'My brave Highlanders, remember your country—remember your forefathers!' And these glories, with all 'the stirring memories of a thousand years,' were not forgotten on that day in the August of 1882 when, under the scion of a gallant house, Cluny the younger, the regiment received its orders of readiness and began to prepare for its departure from the Castle of Edinburgh, while a mighty throb seemed to pervade the heart of the city as its hour of departure approached.

All in its ranks, of course, had friends whom they sorrowed to leave—all save poor Evan Cameron; and all were impatient and full of ardour to join in the coming strife; but none, perhaps, were more impatient than he, for he had to seek forgetfulness—oblivion from his own thoughts—a refuge from his futile regrets—among other scenes for the lost love of one who could never be more to him than a tender memory now.

CHAPTER XVI.

IN THE BELVIDERE.

Shakespeare tells us that men have died and worms have eaten them, but not for love. So Evan Cameron did not die, nor had he any thoughts of dying; but it seemed to his young and enthusiastic heart just then that all which made life worth living for, and all its fulness, splendour, and joy, were over and done with for him.

Of the movements of the Aberfeldie family he knew nothing at that time.

Allan was again on leave, and was to join the regiment on the day of its embarkation in England.

Evan had a longing to see the place where he had last seen Eveline, as her lover, at Maviswood. Memories of the past days at Dundargue came vividly upon him now—of the times when they had wandered in the leafy woods near the old castle, talking sweet nonsense, with happy hearts and laughter that came so readily; when eye spoke to eye and hand thrilled when it touched hand with lingering pressure, and glances were exchanged that, if they meant anything, meant love.

Lord Aberfeldie had been ever kind to him, and a friend of his father; he thought he would like to press the good peer's hand once more before he departed, for the regiment was going far away, to a land from whence he might never return; so, as Evan was an impulsive young fellow, he repaired at once to Maviswood.

He found Mr. Tappleton, the old family butler, airing his figure at the front door when he approached.

Lord Aberfeldie, he was informed, was in London—his lordship was residing with Miss Raymond at Southsea, and Sir Paget was not at home.

'Sir Paget—is he living here?' asked Cameron, with a start.

'Yes, sir, for a few days.'

'And Lady—Lady——' He paused, unable to pronounce the name.

'Is also here,' replied Mr. Tappleton, knowing instantly who he meant; 'but she is out somewhere walking in the grounds.'

Evan gave the butler a couple of cards and turned away. He felt quite startled to find that Sir Paget and his bride were resident at Maviswood, and thought that he could not get away from the vicinity of the house too soon.

Proceeding down the avenue, he passed a narrow, diverging path between high old holly-hedges, the vista of which was closed by a belvidere, or species of pillared alcove, built upon a grassy knoll, and therein, as if in a shrine, stood Eveline.

To pass was impossible. For a moment he stood rooted to the spot, and then, as one in a dream, approached her. To meet her face to face thus, was like something of a dreadful shock to both now.

Eveline was deadly pale and trembling, while her graceful figure looked very slight and girlish in her fresh cambric costume and gipsy hat.

At the very moment of their meeting there, her mind had been full of him.

How had poor Evan borne the tidings of her marriage, and with it the total destruction of their mutual wishes?—mutual hopes they had none.

She had often pondered on this, and wondered how he had heard it, who had told him of it, or if he had seen it in the papers, and how he looked when the sad tidings came. Of the cruel mockery of sending him wedding-cards she knew nothing. Was he striving to forget er? perhaps learning to hate her—oh, not that!—to despise her? nor that, if he knew all.

But they were nothing to each other now, and never could be anything more.

Anon would come other thoughts that were perilous to a young and enthusiastic girl.

Evan Cameron had given himself to her with all his heart, and with all his soul, and he loved her with all the strength of both; and now—now, with another man's wedding-ring upon her finger, she felt unprepared to relinquish that love, for she could not doubt that it must still exist, though he had been cruelly and selfishly treated.

And while all these thoughts had been coursing through her brain he came suddenly before her.

'I pray that he may soon forget me—poor Evan!' had been her frequent thought. 'Why should he think of me more, when he knows of my marriage, and must deem me a pitiful creature.'

Each caught their breath, each clasped their hands as if in mute misery, and the eyes of both were strained, as if the pain of recognition was mingled with the peril of the situation.

Evan thought how pale and transfigured looked the soft face of his lost love!

'I knew not that you where here—I came to visit your father—we march tomorrow—and—and——'

Evan paused breathlessly, though his voice seemed to thrill with passion, and his lips, when they touched her hands—even the hand with the obnoxious wedding-hoop—trembled and quivered like those of a girl.

'Evan,' she said, softly, 'Evan!'

'My darling—my lost darling!' broke from his lips, as he clasped her in his arms, and her slender fingers softly and tremulously caressed his dark and closely-curling hair with something that was almost motherly, or sisterly, in the intensity of its tenderness.

'Oh, Evan,' she whispered, 'may God watch over you, spare you, protect you, and give you some other heart to make you happy.'

It was some solace to Evan's wounded spirit that she had been in a manner—apart from her temporary doubt of himself—forced into her marriage; that her own free will, poor girl, had no hand in the matter.

Clasped to his heart, hers was beating for some moments 'with the wild music of recovered joy, her great dread silenced by her greater passion.'

But to what end was it all?

'This is madness!' exclaimed Evan, as they stood for a minute, hand clasped in hand, and gazing into each other's eyes.

'Madness indeed!' moaned Eveline.

'I am going far away, my darling, and shall never see you again. That I may find a grave in Egypt is the kindest wish you can have for me; and that you will never think but kindly of me in the time to come, is my only and my dearest hope now.'

She was in his arms again—the girl, every tress of whose brown-golden hair was dear to him—every expression of whose eyes and lips, every tone of whose voice, every charm and grace of whose face and form were graven on his inner heart; but what availed all that now?

'You know all now—my secret, and that I was not false to you, Eveline?' said he.

'All,' she replied, hollowly.

'Poor Alice could not come to my quarters in the Castle, consequently I had to meet her somewhere—where you saw us. Poor little soul, she had no one to trust, to—to confide in, save me.'

'And now——'

'She has gone back to her husband—back to my brother in India.'

'Desperate with the idea that you, Evan, had deceived me, I was blind—careless—passive in their hands, and heedless what became of me; and Sir Paget bought me of them—bought me of papa and mamma—as a slave who loathes her buyers and her slavery!' exclaimed Eveline, wildly.

'Such a fate, my darling!'

'Such a fate, indeed!' she whispered through her set teeth. 'But we must part now,' she added, but without withdrawing her hands from his firm clasp.

'A parting bitter as death, Eveline.'

'And as hopeless,' she said, now sobbing heavily.

'Yet, with all its bitterness, this has been a great, an unexpected joy to see you here, to embrace you once again.'

Of one grim fact they could not be oblivious. She was another man's wife, and he had to tear himself away; to lose for ever the sight of that sweet, afflicted face, the tones of that beloved voice, to long again for both, with eager eyes and ears, in the time that was to come.

'Though parted thus, Eveline, you will think of me sometimes—you will remember?'

'For ever and for ever, while my miserable life lasts, Evan.'

'My poor darling! To remember me, to be constant to me in memory, while another's wife.'

'I cannot realise that even now, still less what my life will be in the future, with you not in it.'

A long, clinging kiss and he was gone, while Eveline sank down on the stone seat within the belvidere in a state of semi-consciousness, in which she was discovered by Sir Paget.

CHAPTER XVII.

THE ROUTE.

Few scenes are more stirring than the departure of a regiment for the seat of war, in Scotland, perhaps, more than anywhere else, when it is the departure of a national regiment endeared to the people by historical and warlike associations, combined with those of clanship and kindred.

The last toast at the mess, ere it was broken up, was '*Tir nam Bean, nan Glean, s nan Gaisgaich*;' and now, till more peaceful times, its magnificent and trophied mess-plate was stored away, among it that gigantic silver tripod, with its fluted bowl, weighing eighteen hundred ounces, bearing, with other mottoes, these:—*Na Tir chaisin Buardh son Eiphart* 21 *Mar,* 1801' and—'*O'Chummin Gaidhculach d' on Freicudan Dhu, na* 42 *Regiment.*'

About seven in the morning the pipers of the Black Watch blew the gathering, waking the echoes of that grand old fortress, which is the focus of so much Scottish history, and from the gates of which by sword or spear the tide of war was so often rolled back in the stormy days of old; and now the sound of the pipes found a deeper echo in the hearts of the thousands who were mustering in the streets below to bid the regiment farewell, and wish it God-speed in the land it was going to.

The August morning was a lovely one, and the shadows formed by the golden sunshine lay purple and deep in the glens of the Pentlands, and in the valleys and hollows spanned by the bridges of the city and overlooked by the towering edifices of its terraced streets, amid which rose every spire and pinnacle tipped with ruddy splendour.

The woods and gardens were still in all their summer beauty and greenery, and the corn-fields in the distance were ripe with golden grain over all the sun-lighted landscape. Ere that corn was all gathered, many of those who came gaily forth, mustering to the sound of the pipes, were to find their graves in the sand of the Egyptian desert, where the Black Watch had gathered so many laurels in the wars of other years.

All the city was astir as it had never been since the King's Own left the same fortress for the shores of the Crimea, and the hum of the gathering thousands filled the clear air of the dewy morning.

Cluny trusted in his men, and thus, on this conspicuous morning, no man failed him, and no man was absent from his place in the ranks. The bustle of departure was past; stores had been issued; the grey tropical helmet, with a little crimson hackle worn on the left side, was for a time to supersede the graceful bonnet with its black plumes; valises and haversacks had been packed; rifles and bayonets inspected; the baggage selected and forwarded; and nothing remained now but to march, after sixteen months' residence in the city of the Stuarts.

Cluny had kindly given ample opportunities to his men to take leave of their friends, and it was only for a short time before their departure, that the great palisaded barriers of the Castle were closed at the *tête-du-pont* against all comers, and the human surge that pressed against them.

At last the pipes were heard echoing under that deep archway through which millions of armed men have marched; the brass drums rang under the grim ports of the Half-Moon Battery; the barriers were rolled back, and, with dragoons clearing the way, the Black Watch, in their fighting kits, with grey helmets, white jackets, and dark-green tartans, their colours cased, and all their bayonets glittering in the sun like a rippling stream of steel, came marching down the slope, while cheers rent the air, cheers and shouts, though doubtless many a heavy heart was there, for wives and sweethearts, children and parents, alike were being left behind by those on whose faces they might never look again.

Each man had on his back a valise, tin canteen, and great-coat; his haversack and water-bottle were slung, and attached to a lanyard at his neck each carried a large knife—like the genuine jockteleg of the days of old—and right service-like and purpose-like they all looked.

The officers, who were in blue patrol jackets, with kilt, claymore, and dirk, carried knives of the same kind, together with a haversack, field-glass, and water-bottle.

Dense were the crowds occupying every street, every window and balcony, every coign of vantage, and the whole area through which the regiment marched to the sound of its national and martial music seemed instinct with life, ardour, and enthusiasm.

Many veterans were in the ranks of the regiment—men who had served in Ashanti, and not a few who, as Albany Highlanders, had marched to Candahar and fought in Afghanistan. Their colonel—Cluny the younger, son of that venerable Cluny who is chief of the Macphersons or Clanvurich (the second tribe of the great Clan Chattan), and was once a Black Watchman—rode at their head, and near him marched his favourite sergeant-major, MacNeil, a tall, stately, and tried soldier, who, though he knew not the fate before him, when the hour came, had no fear of facing death, as became one of the Freicudan Dhu.

Evan Cameron, as he marched on, claymore in hand, had a shrewd idea that among the many there whose tender hearts were filled with pity and enthusiasm, would be one who was secretly and inexpressibly dear to himself; and yet, though a kind of mortal pain was in his breast, his heart, despite it all, beat responsive to the cadence of the old familiar march—the regimental quick-step—the same air to which he had so often trod in past times and in other lands; and now, as one in a dream, he saw the seething crowds, the forest of waving hats and handkerchiefs, and all the glorious view on which he was probably looking for the last time—the noble line of Princes Street, steeped in the morning sun, the Calton Hill with its line of towers and battlements, its temples, great stone obelisk, and reproduction of the classic Parthenon of Minerva, Arthur's Seat, and the Craigs, and the old city with its ten-storey houses—each a stone record of the historic past.

He was suddenly roused on seeing Carslogie playfully kiss the basket hilt of his claymore, and wave his hand to a young lady who sat by the side of an elderly gentleman in an open barouche.

She was closely veiled, but Evan's heart leaped in his breast when he recognised Eveline—Eveline by the side of Sir Paget, who waved his hat occasionally, and jerked his bald head about as usual.

'Why was such a girl as that, Allan Graham's sister, sacrificed to that old devil of a fogie?' asked one of the Black Watch of Carslogie, a high-spirited young fellow, who thought it very nice to be in the 42nd, but very nasty to be also in debt, and was now right glad to find himself *en route* for Egypt.

'Why, indeed? you may well ask,' he replied; 'simply because her father is one of the upper ten, and, like all that lot, selfish to the backbone.'

And Cameron's heart endorsed his answer to the full.

Eveline saw him, and for a moment—but a moment only—raised her, veil.

The tale of all she had endured was written in the wistful and mournful expression of her soft hazel eyes, and all who knew her now remarked that, though she sometimes smiled, she never laughed.

She felt her lips quiver and the lines of them tighten, for we may control deep emotion in the eyes, but on the mouth, never.

Her whole heart and soul were concentrated in the effort to appear calm and look on, though her eyes were dim with the tears in which she feared just then to indulge.

'Oh, my darling!' she whispered to herself, again and again, but voicelessly, in her heart. 'My dear love—my brave Evan—I shall never see you again!'

Surreptitiously she concealed her tear-soaked handkerchief in her pocket, and drew forth another—a fresh one redolent of eau-de-Cologne. Quickly though she did it, Sir Paget saw the act, drew his own conclusions therefrom, and thought himself an ass for having accorded her permission to see the Black Watch depart.

Their recent brief meeting—the memory of the passionate kisses that should never have been given or taken—added now to the supremeness of the present moment.

He only appeared to bow to her; but as he gazed with eyes of passionate yearning on her flower-like face, the lips he had kissed so often, the eyes that had so often looked with love into his, and did so now, his heart filled with a wild and desperate longing to take her to his breast and cover her face with kisses again.

But the drums beat, the pipes played loud and high, the crowds cheered, and the forward march went ruthlessly on.

All this fuss of Eveline's, thought Sir Paget, could not be merely for the departure of her brother's regiment!

At last to Eveline's ears the sound of pipe and drum died away in the distance as the barouche was driven homeward to Maviswood; but now the despair in her face and attitude was too palpable not to attract the attention of Sir Paget, who jerked his face forward quite close to hers and regarded her gloomily and in silence.

In all that followed now, Evan Cameron seemed to act mechanically, and to do that which was his duty by mere force of habit, as the regiment marched into the resounding railway station, where he saw the men of his company told-off to compartments; saw the sergeants marking on the footboard of the carriages with chalk the letter of the company; saw the men take off their valises; and ere long the swift special train was sweeping through the dark tunnel that pierces the rocky bowels of Calton Hill, and the Black Watch were fairly off for Egypt again.

How to bear his loss in the long years that were to come, if the fortune of war spared him, was the thought that tortured most the mind of Cameron then, and gave him an emotion of despair.

He remembered the fixed and agonised gaze of Eveline; he remembered, too, the manner in which her spouse had looked grimly on, with an angry, yet not unsatisfied, jerk of the head, as he, no doubt, was thinking they 'had seen the last of Evan Cameron.'

The future! All that was vague to the latter indeed.

CHAPTER XVIII.

'IDIOTS ONLY WILL BE COZENED TWICE.'

It was on an August evening—the sun had not set, but the sky was cloudy and gloomy; the wind was high, and a heavy sea was on at Spithead, and the conservatory in which Olive was lingering and selecting a button-hole of violets and maiden-hair fern for Allan was so dark already that the lamps were lighted in it. She was dressed for a dinner-party, and was looking charming—her best and brightest—as she sang softly to herself and wandered from one shelf of potted flowers to another, when Allan suddenly joined her, with an expression in his face that was full of mingled sadness and excitement, and with a telegram in his hand.

'Allan, what has happened?' she asked, changing colour, and with dire forebodings in her heart.

He caught her hands in his and tried to smile.

'Tell me, why are you so sad?' she asked again.

'Darling,' said he, as he drew her to his breast, 'compose yourself; I have just had great news—bad news you will deem them—to tell you.'

From these few speeches it may be gathered that the cloud that hovered between this pair of lovers had passed away, and that sunshine had come again.

They were at Puddicombe House, a villa of Sir Paget's, which he had lent to Lord Aberfeldie, and from the windows of which, as it overlooked Stokes Bay and Spithead from the Clarence Parade at Southsea, they could daily see the departure of great white 'troopers,' crowded with soldiers—Highlanders, Rifles, and Marines—steaming past the long line of the sea-wall (with all its naval trophies and monuments) *en route* for the shores of Egypt.

There, too, were in view the three forts in the Channel, with Puckpool Battery at Spring Yale, which, with the other in a line on the mainland, would effectually bar an enemy's ship from reaching Portsmouth Harbour. Ponderous indeed are these forts—one in particular, a mass of circular masonry, girt by a black belt of iron armour, pierced with port-holes, through which the great guns of 'the period' may spit out shot and shell; and beyond lies the peaceful Isle of Wight—a charming stretch of sloping land, wooded to the water's edge, and studded with beautiful mansions.

'You have bad news to tell me?' said Olive, as the haunting terror that was ever before her struck a pang to her heart.

'I must rejoin my regiment at once; it leaves the Castle of Edinburgh to-morrow for Egypt, and I am to meet it at Woolwich, where the transport awaits it. Oh, how hard it is to part with you—even for a time,' he added, caressing her, as her head dropped upon his breast; 'to part thus, and unmarried yet, Olive—after all our past folly, jealousies, and waste of time. Speak to me, darling!'

'What can I say, Allan?' replied Olive, piteously, as her tears fell fast.

'We shall not go to this dinner-party at the Port Admiral's, of course. Our last evening must be spent together.'

'Oh, Allan, Allan!'

'Take off those evil diamonds, darling—those stones of ill omen. Why did the mater let you wear them? They are never produced without something happening.'

'And the transport sails—when?'

'On Tuesday evening.'

'So soon—so very soon!'

'My darling—my own—don't weep so,' said he, pressing her closer to his breast, and nestling her face in his neck, while he caressed and tried to soothe her; but the impulsive Olive would neither be soothed nor comforted for a time.

When, however, she became calmer, he said,

'I must leave you for a few minutes. I must telegraph to the adjutant, see the mater, poor soul, and send apologies, as we shall not go to the admiral's to-night.'

He left her; and, sinking into a sofa, she abandoned herself to a stormy fit of weeping and to sad and bitter reflections, and to many unavailing regrets—unavailing now, as they were to be parted so soon; and one grim and harrowing fact stood darkly out amid them all—her affianced lover was going to the seat of war and disease, to face unnumbered perils in that fatal land of Egypt!

A slight sound roused her, and drew her attention to a glass-door of the conservatory that opened to the garden.

A man's face seemed glued against it—a face white and ghastly, apparently regarding her fixedly—the face of Hawke Holcroft, emaciated by dissipation, want, or disease—probably by all three—his shifty eyes bloodshot and wild in expression.

In another moment she would have screamed with terror; but he opened the door, entered, and stood before her.

'I never thought—at least, I was in hope never to see you again,' said Olive, starting up, and recoiling from him.

'Ha—indeed. But in this world are not those always meeting who are better far apart?' was his mocking response.

'What brings you here—what do you want?' asked Olive, gathering courage from desperation, and trembling in her soul lest Allan should return and find this villainous intruder there.

'What do I want! Money. I am, and have been for days, starving.'

'Money I shall not be weak enough to give you again, under any threat or any pressure. The last I gave you cost me dearly,' said Olive, firmly, though terrified to find herself face to face with this would-be assassin again.

'You will not?'

'No.'

'Then give me these jewels—these diamonds,' he said, hoarsely; and, ere she could move or speak, he snatched up the necklace and pendants from a pedestal on which she had placed them, and thrust them into his breast-pocket. 'For a time, now, the work of art I possess shall be withheld from the British public—but for a time only—and in the memory of the time when you loved me, or led me to believe that you did.'

'Insolent—how dare you say so?' she exclaimed.

'You tried to win my heart, and won it, too—you played with me fast and loose, as you did with your cousin, for whom you did not care one doit, then at least, and for whom I believe you care nothing now.'

Olive glanced round her in dismay, for should such words as these, and others that followed them, reach listening ears, she might be lost, and she was powerless to stay the impetuous current of his studiously mischievous speech. Moreover, she did not see what Hawke Holcroft saw behind some towering ferns and other plants—a form, with firm-set teeth and flashing eye, transported by fury, while his feet were rooted to the spot—the face of Allan Graham, who saw and overheard, yet failed to comprehend the situation!

A vindictive desire to separate the lovers if he could, and to humiliate the man he hated, took possession of the diabolical mind of Holcroft, who said,

'Let me kiss your hand, Olive, but once again, ere I leave you—I, whom you loved once so well!'

'Insolent!' exclaimed the girl, impetuously.

But, ere she could resist him or escape, he threw his arms round her, pressed her to his breast, kissed her many times, and then—as Allan sprang forward—he quitted the conservatory, and vanished into the gloom outside, while, with a low wail of horror and distress at the shameful affront put upon her, Olive covered her face with her tremulous hands, and murmured,

'Oh, this is too much to endure!'

'Too much, indeed,' said a voice, as a heavy hand grasped her shoulder, and she was swung round with a force that was almost rude, to meet the white face and flaming eyes of Allan.

'Allan,' she exclaimed, piteously, and held out her hands.

'Stand off and touch me not,' he cried. 'Idiots only will be cozened twice,' he added, unconsciously quoting Dryden.

He gave her an awful and withering glance, and, snatching up a heavy stick, he dashed into the garden after the intruder, whom he saw in the act of escaping by a gate that opened upon the common, across which he fled like a hare, pursued closely by Allan Graham, whom, as an active mountaineer and trained soldier, he was not likely to escape.

The sun had set amid dim and lurid clouds; the evening was gloomy, close, and stormy; the bellowing of the ocean could be heard along the whole line of the sea-wall, from the Spur Redoubt to Southsea Castle. A heavy gale from the offing was rolling the waves in their force and fury upon the shore, where, in anticipation thereof, the boats and bathing machines were all drawn up high and dry upon the shelving shingle. The shipping at anchor were straining on their cables, and sheet lightning, red and fiery, threw forward in black outline from time to time the undulating curves of the Isle of Wight.

But Allan Graham saw none of these things; he only saw the fugitive Holcroft, who ran madly towards the sea-shore, and disappeared round the angle of the East Battery that overhangs the sea, closely followed by his infuriated pursuer.

'What has happened, Olive—speak?' said Lady Aberfeldie, who was completely bewildered by the condition in which she found Olive, and bitterly regretting the absence of her husband, who was then in London; and Olive, feeling now the unwisdom and futility of further concealment, told her all about the power Holcroft had wielded over her by working on her pride, shame, and fear, and how, by direct acting, he had too probably achieved the very end which the evil prompting of a moment had doubtless suggested—the placing of herself in a false position with Allan, and causing a hopeless quarrel and separation between them.

'And now that he has left me thus, auntie, I shall never see him again!' cried Olive, while, burying her face in her hands, she wept bitterly. 'I shall never forget how pallid his poor face became, and how his eyes glared with fury through their unshed tears; and never shall I forget the gaze of tenderness, astonishment, and reproach that came into them as he turned from me in bitter silence.'

'It is very unfortunate,' said Lady Aberfeldie, with difficulty restraining her own tears, though buoyed up by indignation at the daring and insolence of Holcroft; 'but Allan will return in a few minutes, and I shall undertake to explain the whole affair.'

But the time passed on; hour succeeded hour, till midnight struck, and aunt and niece sat watching each other with pale and anxious faces, for there was no appearance of Allan.

They supposed that in his first gust of anger he had gone to some club or hotel, and would, when in a calmer frame of mind, return on the morrow; but the morrow had passed into evening, and he returned no more!

Olive felt that he and she were roughly rent asunder, and likely to drift further and further apart on the stormy sea of life.

And now to account for his non-appearance.

Aware that he had no mercy to expect between the hands of Allan on one side, and those of the police on the other, Hawke Holcroft thought only of escape, and, dreading flight towards the town, in the blindness of his terror or confusion he turned towards the sea, and ran along the summit of the steep, rocky, and abruptly shelving bank that is overlooked by the low earthen-works and square, squat tower of Southsea Castle.

Finding Allan close upon him, so close that he could almost hear his footsteps, amid the bellowing of the wind and booming of the sea that rolled in white foam against the stone parapet wall which was bordered by the narrow pathway he was compelled to pursue, he suddenly turned in blind desperation and levelled a revolver at Allan's head, while a tiger-like fury filled his sallow visage.

It snapped, hung fire, and was struck from his hand by Allan, on which he turned again and fled into the grey obscurity, whither Allan could not follow him now, as the sea with a succession of angry roars was lashing the steep stony bank and hurling its spray over the parapet wall, while wave after wave boiled over all the path the fugitive had to pursue.

Again and again he saw the miserable wretch lose his footing, while the waves tried to suck him down, and again and again, clinging with despairing energy to the edge of the stony path, he strove to recover it.

A low wailing cry of despair escaped him as one wave towering higher than all the rest—perhaps a tenth wave, if there be such a thing—enveloped him in its foamy flood and sucked him furiously downward in its back-wash, amid which he seemed to struggle feebly as a fly might have done.

Once or twice Allan saw his head bobbing amid the white foam and his upthrown hands, that had nothing to clutch at, till the waves dashed him again and again, as if in wild sport, among a row of great wooden dolphins which are placed in the shingle there to break the fury of the incoming sea, and stand up like a line of gigantic teeth, and in less than a minute Hawke Holcroft vanished from sight!

Then a long breath escaped Allan.

'The sea has done it not I, though richly did he merit at my hands the fate he has met,' thought he, as he hurried away to alarm the sentinels and castle guard; but all too late to succour Holcroft in any way or even to search for his body.

Darkness had set in now, the fury of the sea was increasing, and if Hawke Holcroft was found at all, it would be as a drowned man, with the fatal diamonds in his possession, when the tide ebbed and the long stretch of seaweed and shingle was left dry.

But he might never be found at all, and lie, as the skeletons are still lying there, among the timbers of the *Royal George*.

Allan knew that he was due with his regiment at Woolwich on the morrow, and, being full of rage and bitter disappointment with disgust at the whole of this recent event—too full to have explanations with his mother, or hear aught that Olive Raymond might, as he naturally thought, be artful enough to advance, perhaps to brazen out—intent only on quitting the scene and, if possible, of forgetting a situation so degrading and repugnant to his pride—he resolved to write to his father renouncing his cousin for ever; and, throwing himself into a cab, drove straight to the railway station and took the first train to London.

Hence it was that he returned to Puddicombe House no more.

And as the train swept clanking along the line, amid the monotony of its sound the words of Olive's song, with what he deemed her accursed raillery underlying them, came gallingly back to his memory, with painful reiteration,

'I know a maiden fair to see,
Take care!
She can both false and friendly be,
Beware, beware!
Trust her not. She is fooling thee.'

'And for what a wretched creature she has dared to fool me!' he thought, while a bitter malediction hovered on his lips.

In due time, with all his comrades of the Black Watch, he found himself on board the *Nepaul*, and, after she had steamed out of the Albert Dock, amid the deafening cheers of thousands, even amid all the bustle and high military enthusiasm that surrounded him, he felt half mad with grief, mortification, and fury.

Night and day his mind was full of angry and bitter dreams; a conviction of Olive's guilt and the shame of her discovery were ever before him.

Brave young Allan Graham was stricken to the heart; yet he bore himself graciously and gallantly, though a conviction grew strong in his mind that he would find his grave in the land he was going to.

CHAPTER XIX.

IN THE LAND OF THE PHARAOHS.

Ismailia, by the Lake of Timsah, lay steeped in sunshine, while the regiments of the Highland Brigade, for the second time, after the lapse of eighty years, landed upon Egyptian soil again.

Built equi-distant from Port Said and Suez, this new town protects the outlet of the second canal, which carries the supply of fresh water from the Nile near Cairo to the Isthmus. In 1862 the place where it stands was a scene of sandy desolation. Seven years later saw a brilliant little French town in existence with a broad quay, bordering the lake, with hotels, cafés, a theatre where vaudevilles were acted, a street of well-stocked shops, a public garden with a fountain spouting Nile water in the Place Champollion, the telegraph wires overhead, and the bells of a Christian church ringing, where, but a short time before, the wandering Bedouin, the nomadic dweller in tents, the child of the desert, with glittering spear and floating burnous, urged his camel on its solitary way from Ramses to Serapium.

The heat was intense, and to the eyes of the Scottish mountaineers the scenery about Ismailia seemed intensely monotonous. Cloudless skies of the deepest and richest blue formed a contrast to the vast expanse of yellow sand that stretched far, far away till lost in hazy distance, but the desert is susceptible of many shades and changes of colour.

It is said that at Ismailia the stranger can very fully realise the purity, the balm, and beauty of the Egyptian night, especially if seated over wine and a cigar in the Hôtel des Voyageurs, where he may watch the Lake of Timsah, and so varied are the tints of the latter in the light of the red sun setting in the west, amid a lurid glow of gold and crimson, that it looks like three lakes; towards the canal that leads to Serapium it seems a deep blue; where the ships are grouped near Ismailia, its wavelets seem silver with gold, while the moon comes slowly up like a silver dawn, and rosy tints yet linger when the sun has gone abruptly down.

But no time was given to the Highlanders either to study scenery or artistic effects, even if so disposed. Each regiment was rapidly formed in column—every officer and man in his fighting kit, with tropical helmet, haversack, and water bottle; the men with their valises and greatcoats, and the march began towards the desert where the Egyptians of Arabi awaited them at Tel-el-Kebir.

Little was talked of then but the recent cavalry fight at Kassassin, where our Life Guards swept the ranks of Arabi's infantry, and where a horde of wild Bedouins, who had been hovering near the field like birds of prey, after their departure poured in to strip and rob the dead and wounded of both armies, killing all who were able to resist.

The mess—or regiment rather, as there was no mess now—saw that Allan Graham had come back a sorely changed man, who had hours of evident depression alternated by furious hilarity—not the man's old style at all; but his world, like Hamlet's, was 'out of joint.' The conduct of Olive Raymond yet remained a profound, an unexplained and exasperating mystery to him; but he felt, how bitterly, that love lives even after trust and faith are dead and buried; and now that he was so far, far away from her, dreams of a yearning and sorrowful kind, with many stinging thoughts, that he feared would never leave him, filled his mind as he marched at the head of his company towards the darkening desert.

In his looks and manner, Evan Cameron, like others, read a marked yet undefinable change; his bearing now was occasionally haughty and reserved; at other times his eyes seemed strangely sad. What could have happened? Cameron did not ask, and as yet Allan said nothing about it; and, sooth to say, in his own thoughts of Eveline, the former had cause to be sad enough too.

His memories were ever of the days at Dundargue, and the chance parting in the belvidere at Maviswood; and again her kisses, the touch of her little caressing hands, with her voice came vividly to him.

In some of the last papers that had reached the transport, *viâ* the Continent, he could see that she was leading a life of outward gaiety. Could he doubt that it was otherwise than outward? He gathered a sombre satisfaction from the thought, and then strove to set it aside as selfish.

Why should she not enjoy balls and flowers-shows, races and regattas, the drawing-room at Buckingham Palace, and other brilliant gatherings? Yet as he read of these things a frown of mingled anger, sorrow, and even mockery gathered on his brow in spite of himself.

In the same papers Allan could discover no trace of any body having been cast upon the beach either at Southsea or the shore of the Isle of Wight, and hence he supposed that the remains of the drowned Holcroft must have been taken out to sea.

The Highland enthusiasm, the warlike spirit that blazed up within him, kept him from a great despair, for latterly his love for Olive had become a part of his own existence.

The novelty of the land in which our new campaign had opened, the incessant watchfulness, the time and attention each duty brought with it, all gave him a recklessness as to life and as to fear of death, that after a time won him the involuntary admiration of the Black Watch and the whole Highland Brigade.

Just as the sun set, the bugles sounded a 'halt' after a march of six miles, but six terrible miles they were, for at every step the Highlanders sank ankle-deep in the soft and sun-dried sand.

All around that halting-place a sea of the latter seemed to stretch in every direction, bare and desolate, save where Ismailia lay, its edifices looking inky, black, and opaque in outline against the orange and primrose sky; and black looked the masts of the transports as they rose like a forest amid the waters of the Lake of Timsah.

When the first bivouac was formed at El-Magfar, the bare-kneed Highlanders, each rolled in his blanket on the soft sand, slept comfortably enough; but with morning came the first instalment of misery, when the heavy dew that soaks everything left them cold and stiff, and longing even for the fierce unclouded sun again.

'A devil of a country this,' said Carslogie. 'By day it is too hot to eat, to act, or even to think; and at night it is too cold to sleep or think of anything but the bitter cold itself.'

And but for the hot tea made for all over-night, when the brigade first came to its camping-place, some injury to health must have ensued; but the men were too weary to eat even a biscuit, of which each carried a two days' supply in the canvas haversack that formed his only pillow.

Before the sun was up, Allan rose from the sand and looked about him. Under the starlight the Highland bivouac—for camp it was not—presented a curious sight, as the men lay in ranks, each rolled in his blanket, beside the piles of arms; the sentinels of the out-piquets on the way to Tel-el-Mahuta standing dark and motionless against the blue of the sky, looking in kilt and helmet like the statues of ancient Romans.

To get a little warmth ere the pipers blew the 'rouse,' he walked a short distance from where the men of his company lay, and near a fragment of ruined wall, beside which grew a patch of those prickly plants (round which hillocks of sand occasionally gather), and a solitary gum-tree grew, he found, rolled up in a burnous, and evidently concealing himself in dread and fear, a Bedouin. There was a small palm-grove near Magfar; why did he not seek hiding there?

'Hallo, my man,' thought Allan, 'what are you lurking here for?—mischief, no doubt.'

He drew his claymore, supposing the lurker could be but a spy who had crept within our chain of sentries; but the wild son of the desert raised his hands deprecatingly, and, opening his burnous, showed that he was perishing from a dreadful wound—a sword cut that had laid open his right shoulder and breast.

Allan put his brandy-flask to the sufferer's lips, raising his head as he did so, and then addressed him inquiringly. Allan had picked up some Arabic in India, and thus could understand the Bedouin, who informed him that he had been wounded thus, by one of those sons of Anak, our Life-guardsmen, in the charge at Kassassin.

'An Egyptian, by jingo!' exclaimed Carslogie, who came up at that moment. 'Are you about to become a studier of humanity?'

'Well, Cuvier was great in the study of wasps, and so forth. Why shouldn't I study Egyptians?' replied Allan, grimly, 'and this poor devil seems to have been wounded in the affair at Kassassin the other day.'

'You understand him, then?'

'Perfectly. Please bring one of the staff surgeons quickly; he must have been lying here when we took up our ground over-night.'

The Bedouin, whose astonishment that he was not butchered on the instant was great, stared alternately at Allan and at Carslogie, who was a young fellow of the best style, one whose fine face even the hideous tropical helmet (which is such an appalling substitute for the graceful feather bonnet) could not spoil. His figure was slight and elegant, his features clearly cut and refined, and his bright brown chestnut hair was close and curly.

The Bedouin was a perfect type of his race, and, save that he had a good Remington rifle slung over his back, was not much changed in habit, nature, or turn of thought from his ancestors of the tribe of Ishmael.

Though weakened now by suffering and great loss of blood, he seemed spare of figure and light of limb, well-formed and active, tall, but whether thirty or forty years old it was impossible to say. He had a long, thin, and expressive countenance, with glittering black eyes and teeth of pearly whiteness. His colour was a dusky brown, his hair black and wiry.

He was evidently a Bedouin of the desert, as the two ends of the scarlet shawl which formed his turban hung down upon the shoulder, to distinguish him from the Arabs of other tribes. He was clad in a thick dark brown baracan of wool, which served as a dress by day and a bed by night, over which was a robe with wide sleeves.

When the doctor was dressing his wound, which was certainly a terrible sword-cut, his richly embroidered girdle was seen, and this announced him to be a sheikh, and such he was proved to be, as Allan gathered from him that his name was Zeid el Ourdeh, the sheikh of a tribe near Jebel Dimeshk, between the desert and the disused railway to Heliopolis, 'the City of the Sun;' and as he lay there in his picturesque costume, with a group of wondering Highlanders, in their dark kilts and white helmets, gathered round him, and the blood-red sun in the distance, coming swiftly up out of the dry sand of the yellow desert, as it seemed, Allan thought what a subject was the whole for the pencil of an artist.

The Bedouin was on the point of fainting, so great was the agony occasioned by the dressing of his wound; but a mouthful from Allan's flask revived him more than it would have done one usually accustomed to such stimulants.

'Some sick men are going back to the rear at Ismailia,' said Allan. 'Carslogie, please to order the ambulance people to come this way. I'll send this unfortunate creature to the Third Field Hospital.'

Carslogie paused to scrape a vesta and light a cigar, which he proceeded to puff with a sigh of satisfaction.

'Quick, Carslogie,' cried Allan. 'We have no time to lose. The bugles will sound immediately.'

And Carslogie went on his way with the air of a man who thought the world would be none the worse for having a Bedouin the less in it.

In his own language, and in terms peculiarly his own, Allan could make out that the sheikh was thanking him in a low and earnest voice, and adding that while life lasted he 'would always deem him as a brother. You infidels are powerful as the genii of old; you can flash a light at night brilliant as that of the sun at noon; you have another light that springs from the unseen air. I have seen it in the streets of Cairo' (no doubt referring to gas); 'and you can send your thoughts from land to land under the sea more swiftly than even the Afrite did in the days of Solomon; and I fear that from your hands the Egyptians will suffer such chastisement as fell on the people of Noah, of Ad, and of Thamud,' he added, wearily and sadly, as his head fell on one side.

A party of the ambulance had now come, and Allan informed him that he was to be sent to Ismailia. He did more; he placed some money in his hand wherewith to procure necessaries, and, while the eyes of the Bedouin gleamed with gratitude, his brown mahogany and attenuated fingers closed avariciously and tightly on such an unusual gift as coins.

''Pon my soul, Allan Graham,' said Carslogie, 'considering how these rascals treated our wounded at Kassassin, your humanity, to say the least of it, seems to me to be a little misplaced.'

'Perhaps; but I cannot help it. I feel a little tender-hearted just now,' said Allan, with a smile, as the wounded Bedouin—of whom he had not seen the last—was borne away.

The pipes struck up, and once more the columns began a ten-miles' march to Mahsameh. The Gordon Highlanders were in advance, the Camerons next, then came the Highland Light Infantry, and then the Black Watch, all toiling through the soft, deep sand. These splendid regiments were all marching in massed columns, at one pace interval, the cavalry moving with them collaterally on one flank, and the artillery on the other, clattering along, with spunges, buckets, spare wheels, and forge waggons—all forming a grand, impressive spectacle in the midst of the wide Egyptian desert.

To Scottish soldiers, who are usually so well-grounded in their Bible history, the soil they were treading, if the toil made it disgusting on one hand, memory made it full of deep interest on the other. They knew that they were already in, or were approaching, the Land of Goshen, where, by the tasks they had conned at school and those which their ministers superintended, they were aware that they were nigh unto the place where Jacob dwelt of old, that he might be near to Joseph, who lived at Pharaoh's court; near to the place where father and son met, and where we still find Rameses, which was built by the Israelites in the days of their bondage; and, as our soldiers marched on, some there were who recalled these things to each other, as their minds went back to the village kirk, whose bells awoke the echoes of green and lonely glens, and to the firesides of their fathers, when expounding on these things on Saturday night, when the 'big ha' Bible' was produced; and, though they might yawn wearily over such matters at home, these scriptural names and localities had a very different effect upon them now.

CHAPTER XX.

THE MARCH THROUGH GOSHEN.

On, and on, and on, through the same kind of Egyptian landscape—tame, barren, and insipid—so terribly vapid and flatly horrid, when compared with the Salvatoresque hills and glens of their native land—the naked plain, bounded by occasional hillocks at vast distances—the toilsome march of the Highlanders continued. Yet there are luxuriant plains in some parts of the Land of Goshen.

Sometimes date-trees were seen, with trunks bare and slender, or mud-walled wigwams on the causeways; but it is a land that, with all its vast antiquity and religious associations, of which no poet has ever sung. 'What, indeed, could an Egyptian sing on the reed of Gesner or Theocritus?' asks Volney. 'He sees neither limpid streams, nor verdant lawns, nor solitary caves; and is equally a stranger to valleys, mountain-sides, and impending rocks.' Miss Martineau is almost the only traveller who claims for Egypt the attributes of the picturesque and varied in beauty!

And there were incessant swarms of scorpions, gnats, and more especially of flies—one of the many plagues of Egypt—which were so numerous that it was impossible to eat the dry ration biscuits without the chance of swallowing these pests also.

More than once, on the summit of a sandy hillock, there would appear, sharply defined against the clear blue sky, the picturesque figure of a mounted Bedouin, with his white burnous floating about him, a tall, reed-like spear, or a long musket slung by his side—a man unchanged in aspect or ideas from his nomadic forefathers, who saw the mailed Crusaders toiling on their way to Jerusalem—gazing with stolid wonder at the marching columns in a costume so strange, with bare knees, white sporrans, and kilts of dark-green tartan waving at every step; while on the hot and breathless air there was borne towards him the hoarse and shrill music of the pipes—the same wild music that, eighty years before, woke the echoes of the Pyramids and of the streets of Grand Cairo.

But what land in the world has not echoed to their music?

All our soldiers were more or less full of enthusiasm—anxious to get at Arabi—to grapple with the enemy, 'and get the business over,' as they phrased it; though it is doubtful if they quite believed in Sir Garnet Wolseley's apparently boastful prediction that the war would be ended by the 16th of that month, September.

In the exuberance of their spirits, many chorussed merrily when the pipes ceased, which was seldom, lilting as, a writer says, only 'the song-loving Scots' can do, as in the days when their country was redolent of song, when the milk-maid sang some old chant to her cows in field or byre, when the house-wife span at her ingle-neuk, when the reapers filled the harvest-field with melody, and the ploughman in winter when he turned the glistening furrows over the lea.

And now and anon the Bedouin scouts would wheel their horses round and vanish ere our cavalry could reach them to bear to Tel-el-Kebir the terrible tidings, as some said, 'that devils in petticoats' were coming, and, as others asserted, 'devils with beards down to their knees.'

Every man had one hundred rounds of ball-cartridge and his bottle filled with water from the Canal, called by the soldiers jocularly 'Egyptian soup,' from its hue and quality; thus a ration of rum, when it was served out, proved very acceptable, though some there were who did not much affect the cold tea, and Allan could not help smiling at a little argument that ensued between Corporal MacSnish of his company and one of the Scripture-readers, who, to their honour, be it said, kept up with the troops, went under fire with them, and after the conflict did all in their power to alleviate the sufferings of the wounded.

'Don't grumble, corporal,' said the Scripture-reader, 'though I know it is a soldier's privilege. He who paints the lilies of the field and feeds the sparrow will supply all you want.'

'Oich, I hope so, whateffer; but a corporal of the Black Watch is worth a good many sparrows, I can tell you, and as for the cold tea—ugh!'

'Better for you than all the liquor in the world, my man,' said the Scripture-reader.

'Even the worst whusky, whateffer, would be better to my mind; and we have Scripture for it that we should not drink water alone.'

'Indeed!' said the reader, doubtfully.

'Yes,' urged the corporal, who knew his Bible well; 'are we not told in Maccabees, chapter xv. and verse 39, that "it is hurtful to drink wine or water alone, as wine mingled with water is pleasant and delighteth the taste?"'

'For all that,' replied the Scripture-reader, 'I agree with Sir Garnet that water is alone the drink for man.'

'Yet the only man that Holy Writ records as ever asking for it, didn't get it.'

'Who was *he*?'

'Dives, and we all know where *he* was then. Scripture again!' said the corporal, with a smirk on his sharp Highland face, and thinking he had decidedly the best of the argument.

During a mid-day halt on this march, some of the troops constructed out of blankets and rifles with fixed bayonets erections like gipsy tents, to shelter them from the blazing heat of the sun, and a singular kind of encampment they presented.

With ship biscuits and tinned meat and some brandy to flavour their cold tea, Allan Graham, Cameron, Carslogie, and some other officers of the corps made themselves as comfortable as they could under shelter of their impromptu tents, and many were even jolly, especially Carslogie, who was rather a noisy and irrepressible fellow.

Stretched on the sand with his tropical helmet tilted back on his head, he drank his 'cold tea,' as he called it, though it was stiff half-and-half grog, and proffered his cigar-case to all.

'Isn't this jolly!' he exclaimed. 'Instead of this, we might have been out in the blazing open.'

Then he struck up a verse of a song to the air of the 'Garb of Old Gaul,' and composed by an anonymous writer, though he hinted it was Mr. John Bright:—

'They talk of a good time, when warfare shall cease,
And the nations hobnob o'er a big pipe of peace,
And the lion and the lamb in auriferous mead
On bills of exchange in beatitude feed.
But keep your powder dry, my boys, and keep your bayonets keen;
The world can't do without us yet, nor will it soon, I ween!
Then stern and true, where work's to do, we'll do it as we can,
And shoulder to shoulder still march in the van!'

'The good time predicted seems a long way off yet,' he added, with a sigh, to find that the last of his grog was gone, for after a hot morning's march it was, as he said, 'quite a Sybaritish luxury.' 'Well, well, a little time will find us face to face with Arabi, and we shall exchange the fleshpots of Egypt for those of the old country.'

This was the 11th of September, and the march was resumed at five in the evening for the head-quarters at Kassassin, where the column found its tents pitched. Allan shared his with Cameron, and, like their comrades, they proceeded to make themselves as comfortable as they could; but it soon became known that on the morrow the Highland Brigade was to lead in the night attack upon the formidable entrenchments of Arabi Pasha at Tel-el-Kebir.

'The last bugle some of us may ever hear will sound at six to-morrow evening,' said Allan, as he and Cameron, after a picnic kind of repast, lay on the floor of the tent and smoked their Havanas, with their jackets open, and minus collars and ties, for the evening was hot then, though cold and dew came together the moment the sun went down, and then there was no light in the tent save those of the stars.

'Listen to Carslogie singing in his tent; no sombre reflections seem to come to him,' said Cameron.

'Some of us, of course, will lose the number of our mess, as the sailors say,' said Allan again, after a pause.

'Well, it is not a cheerful thought, Allan,' said Cameron; 'but life is not particularly rosy with me just now, so I am just the fellow to have a charmed one when under fire again to-morrow.'

'There is a history in all men's lives, Cameron, it is said. Well, there is a devil of a lot in mine—more than I care for.'

'You have long seemed rather low in spirit.'

'I have reason,' replied Allan, while that inexpressible longing to talk of himself and his sorrows, which seizes upon men now and then, came upon him, and he related to Cameron the whole story of his engagement with his cousin, his doubts and fears—the intrusions and outrageous insults put upon them both by Hawke Holcroft, who seemed to wield some degrading and mysterious power once—a power that was ended now; 'and,' he added, after his narrative was ended, 'I trust under heaven never to look upon her false fair face again!'

Cameron heard his strange story in silent amazement.

'Can all this not be explained?' he asked.

'I want no explanation; I have been degraded enough,' replied Allan, bitterly.

Cameron, strangely enough, had never, as yet, even to his early friend and comrade, made any reference to what the latter fully knew—his love for Eveline: and never once had her name escaped him during the long voyage in the Nepaul from Woolwich to Ismailia, nor even on the march towards the enemy.

Poor Cameron had thought, what was the use of speaking of that matter now, when all was hopeless—all over, and for ever, between them? But now, encouraged or melted by Allan Graham's new confidence in himself, he said,

'With reference to the risks we run tomorrow, I am glad that I set my house in order, did so, indeed, before we marched from Edinburgh.'

'How?'

'About Stratherroch, or what remains of it.'

'In what way, Evan?'

We must all die sooner or later—a soldier sooner, perhaps, than a civilian; so by will, if aught happens to me—I have left the old place—tower and hill, wood, glen, and water, to—to Eveline—I mean to Lady Paget.'

'Good heavens! To Eveline!' exclaimed Allan, his face full of a surprise that was unseen in the starlight and darkened bell tent.'

'Yes.'

'Have you no one else?'

'None save my brother Duncan, who has himself a large fortune—none whom I love as—as I love her,' added Cameron, in a very broken voice.

'Poor Evan! I always suspected—indeed, knew of it.'

'You did?'

'Yes, Evan.'

'And—and your sister.'

'She loved you.'

'My God!—yet was sacrificed to another.'

They wrung each other's hands in the dark, and both remained silent for a time, each full of his own thoughts, and in the gloom seeing nothing but the end of the other's cigar.

'Sir Paget is so rich that he will think little of Stratherroch, even when cleared of its heavy encumbrances,' said Evan.

'But he may think rather wrathfully of the donor, though I trust and hope he may never get it. And now, good-night, Evan. I have to parade the inlying picquet. Get some sleep if you can, old fellow—we'll need all our metal on the morrow.'

And Allan, taking his dirk and claymore, hurried away full of thought, for, if his friend really fell, this odd bequest of Stratherroch might compromise his sister with her elderly spouse, and it was impossible to make any change, circumstanced as they were then.

'It is said that "every man has a history, and that every man outlives it,"' thought Allan; 'I wonder how it will be with poor Evan and me. And now to parade the picquet, with that paragon of sergeant-majors, M'Neill. Picquets parade at sunset—here, however, the sun sets before we have time to think of it. But the fight to-morrow will be to Evan and me—for a time, at least—what opium was to De Quincey and the author of the "Ancient Mariner." Fool, fool, fool that I am, to think of *her* here at all!'

He left Evan Cameron inspired by a mingled emotion of gratitude and satisfaction, for Evan now knew and felt certain that, had Eveline been in Allan's gift, she might have been his bride ere this; and with this conviction in his mind he strove to court sleep, while roused ever and anon, as in India, by the wild cry of the jackal.

Sir Garnet Wolseley had now come up, the brigade of guards also, and the whole strength of the British force was concentrated at Kassassin, the place of our cavalry victory, where our horse so gallantly charged and swept, sword in hand, through the brigades of Egyptian guns in the dark.

With the next day's dawn those officers, who, like the Master of Aberfeldie, Cameron, and others, advanced beyond a palm wood that grew near the camp, could distinctly see with their field-glasses, against the bright orange tint shed on the sky by the up-coming sun, the strong earthworks of Tel-el-Kebir crowning the hillocks, and manned by more than twenty thousand regular troops—the flower of the army of Arabi, who commanded them in person; and when the sun rose higher the infantry could be seen lining the trenches, with all their serried bayonets flashing in the sunshine.

Beyond these formidable earthworks the Egyptian camp could be seen in the distance spreading far away an almost unbroken line of tents, which, if they had all occupants, betokened the presence of a very great force indeed, as more than one reconnoitring officer remarked to another.

Many were full of disappointment lest there might be no fighting after all, as the preceding morning the sound of heavy firing had been heard in the rear of the Egyptian position, and there seemed a prospect of internal dissension facilitating a dissolution of the whole enemy's force.

Others more wisely suggested that Arabi was only practising his artillery to obtain the range in case his position was turned and attacked in the rear, though some asserted that the deep booming of the guns was too steady and continuous for mere practice of that nature.

The British troops had only a five days' reserve of provisions, but it was generally known that the country was rich and full of subsistence beyond the lines of Tel-el-Kebir, and that we would carry these no man under Wolseley doubted. Moreover, he had with him sixty of the finest pieces of cannon in the world.

The day passed on, and evening drew nigh, the eventful day of the 12th September, when every man was prepared to 'do or die!' Higher and higher beat every heart. At six p.m. the 'fall in' was sounded far along the lines, and quietly, as if upon parade at home, that stately soldier M'Neill, sergeant-major of the Black Watch, paraded and posted the markers for the various companies of his corps, 'dressing' them with his usual accuracy.

The orders were brief but emphatic. Perfect silence was to be maintained for the march, and, as the place was to be carried in grand old British style at the point of the bayonet, on no account was an order to load to be issued.

Each man carried a hundred rounds of ball with one day's provisions, and his tin water-bottle filled with cold tea. The tents were struck, and the baggage piled for conveyance to the rear, in case of a reverse, which no man thought possible.

The blood-red sun went swiftly down westward of the point of attack beyond Zagazig, darkness fell as swiftly over the desert and the triple lines of canal that flow between both Mahsameh and Abassa, and then our army, fourteen thousand strong, including foot, horse, and artillery, began in silence the midnight march for Tel-el-Kebir, the last march as it proved to many a brave young fellow.

As the regiment moved off, Allan thought of Evan Cameron's communication over-night, and an irrepressible regret and anxiety took possession of him, as he had an unaccountable presentiment that his friend was doomed to fall in the coming strife. Of himself he never thought at all.

END OF THE SECOND VOLUME.

CPSIA information can be obtained
at www.ICGtesting.com
Printed in the USA
LVHW030241040223
738616LV00006B/989

9 789356 908123